Trends in Energy Trading, Transaction and Risk Management Software

A PRIMER

Catalog-in-Publication Data

Dr. Gary M. Vasey and Andrew Bruce
Trends in Energy Trading, Transaction and Risk Management Software – A Primer
ISBN 1-4196-3355-4

Design by Inreason Media
www.inreason.com

Printed in the United States of America

First Edition 2006

Trends in Energy Trading, Transaction and Risk Management Software

A PRIMER

Edited by

Dr. Gary M. Vasey

VP, Macroenergy Analysis,

UtiliPoint International, Inc.

&

Andrew Bruce

VP, Trading and Risk Management

UtiliPoint International, Inc.

CONTENTS

DEDICATION

To all we have worked with and learned from through the years our sincere thanks. It's a small industry we work in that is made all the more enjoyable by its community and all of those familiar faces.

FOREWORD

By Jon T. Brock
Chief Operating Officer
UtiliPoint International, Inc.

In the late 1980's I went to work in information technology at Amerada Hess. I was based in the exploration and production unit and was therefore focused on operational systems. We were involved in an exciting project of automating the field with something called Andersen's TOW (The Oilfield Workstation by Verticomp) and integrating it into Price Waterhouse's PREMAS system. Those two "state-of-the-art" systems were replacing a 1969 era PL-1 code production accounting system in use at Amerada Hess. We would fly to Lafayette, LA, implement the field systems, test them, integrate them back into PREMAS in the home office, and train the users in the field, also known as lease operators or "pumpers." We would also enjoy the local flavor, especially when the EVP of Production would check-in on us. Dinners at Cajun restaurants would be 4-5 hour affairs. I thought I had died and gone to heaven. Then I would hear the EVP complain how things had changed since the "boom" days of oil and gas. We really weren't enjoying ourselves compared to where the market had been. Wow, I thought, things were better than this?

Eventually I ended up in IT at an electric utility, the last great monopolistic legacy of employment security, right? Wrong. Soon upon my arrival the utility embarked on a massive consolidation effort to create a shared services company. It soon learned the cruel realities of balancing the rate payer with the investor as the regulatory forces reduced rates at the utility to equal the savings achieved. Then deregulation occurred, or kind of occurred.

Markets change, of this we can be certain. Look at the two companies that sold Amerada Hess TOW and PREMAS. Where is Andersen? Where is Price Waterhouse? Today the comfort zone of utilities is eroding, as powerful external drivers (e.g., globalization, political and regulatory climate, technological advances, market fluctuations, corporate governance and accounting reform, etc.) and what this book's editors term "dislocation events" have converged to mark the dawning of a new epoch in the corporate world generally and the energy industry specifically.

If I were to break down a timeline of events since the early nineties, three main periods of activity in the utility industry are defined:

Regulatory "Bliss" (1992-1997)

- 10-year planning was the "norm" for utilities—remember IRP?
- Regulatory recovery was the name of the game
- Biggest concern was EMFs from transmission lines

Retail "Craze" (1998-2001)

- Utilities search for the "killer app.
- Customer Relationship Management (CRM) a "must"
- Product development searches for the "caller-id of utilities"
- Shift from account or meter centric to customer-centric
- Must serve 10 million customers or you will not survive

"Back-to-the-Basics" (2002-2006)

- Utilities re-trench by selling off non-core assets
- Realize that they are one of the most asset-intensive industries in the world
- Focus on operational excellence as opposed to marketing excellence

Unfortunately, many utilities began 2002 by interpreting "back-to-basics" as doing nothing—cutting budgets and reducing staff. Today, many utilities have abandoned that definition and replaced it with strategic investing in what is core—maintaining an industry that is the most asset-intensive industries in the world. Managing the assets has always been done by utilities, but with new technology and a renewed interest, it is becoming an investment priority in 2006.

Not to be outdone are the new clean-tech initiatives related to emissions in the sector. This industry has basically moved from natural gas, to electric power, to merchant, to financial, and now to asset-backed and emission related. Boring? Not at all! Read on.

As recognized thought leaders in the industry, Dr. Vasey and Mr. Bruce's characterization of dislocation events and trends moving forward in the energy trading, transaction and risk management industry is fascinating, illuminating, and provides direction for those of us navigating the changing tides of the utility and energy industries.

INTRODUCTION

Energy trading, transaction and risk management (ETRM) software is that software required by firms to support the business processes related to buying or selling, moving and managing any energy commodity. UtiliPoint estimates the total market for ETRM software as perhaps around $30-60 million annually in North America alone. But the ETRM software market is still relatively immature and continues to evolve rapidly with more than 65 vendor provided solutions in the market and between a 40 percent to 60 percent penetration rate for vendor-provided software. The ETRM software market has mirrored the changes that have taken place over the last 15-years in wholesale energy markets with boom periods followed by slowdowns as the industry absorbed structural or regulatory changes. UtiliPoint calls these periods of industry change dislocation events. To understand the ETRM software landscape, one needs to understand the industry's history of change and in particular, how these dislocation events impacted the vendor community and its software products.

Today, when one looks at the installed base of ETRM software, it is like reading the history of the industry. Each dislocation event brought new requirements, new solutions and vendors and sometimes sounded the death knell for other solutions and vendors. Merger and acquisition activity between vendors has also occurred such that some software products were phased out and others had a shortened shelf life. However, it has been the pace of industry change with its rapidly shifting requirements and overall complexity that has meant that the ETRM software space has remained so dynamic and somewhat immature. Replacement rates for ETRM software are very high as compared to other classes of energy software. For example, UtiliPoint research shows a once in ten-year cycle of replacement for Customer Information Systems (CIS) in utilities but a 2-3 times per 10-year replacement rate for ETRM software.

In an era of increased financial scrutiny, corporate governance and risk controls, ETRM solutions have become even more important components in meeting regulatory requirements. Legislation such as the Sarbanes-Oxley Act and the recommendations of the Committee of Chief Risk Officers (CCRO) have been followed by increased emphasis on risk controls by organizations such as S&P. This has meant that business processes in the area of wholesale energy trading have had to be examined and bolstered and that the ETRM software supporting those business processes has come under increased scrutiny too. ETRM software now has to provide not just the complex functionality to support those business processes but also the controls required by the auditors and executive management.

ETRM software is a mission critical component in a company's software inventory today but it also needs to be an integrated component in the overall software architecture. For that reason, a new round of ETRM software development has and is taking place as vendors migrate their solutions to new, more flexible and scalable architectures that can provide built in connectivity.

As the importance of ETRM software grows, so too has the ability to implement the solutions selected properly. As a result of the complexity of the industry and its requirements, ETRM software has to be built to be highly configurable. While configurability provides users with a powerful and flexible solution it also increases the complexity involved in implementing that software. UtiliPoint research suggests that in the past, implementation of ETRM has been highly variable in terms of its success and has had a high failure rate. As many of the vendors mature their services to support implementation assisted by a growing number of knowledgeable third-party consultants and services firms, the emphasis on implementation processes and procedures is growing. Buyers of third-party ETRM software also need to better understand the complexity and magnitude of ETRM software implementation in order to dedicate the proper budget and resources to these projects.

This book draws upon the body of research and analysis by UtiliPoint consultants in the Trading & Risk Management Practice. While some of the material has appeared as IssueAlerts or as Whitepapers, some of it is also new and updated. The content has been carefully edited and updated to present to the reader as complete as possible picture of the ETRM software segment today. This book was not designed to be a detailed review of requirements for ETRM software since that varies significantly on a company by company basis. Instead, this book is a primer for anyone who wishes to understand the ETRM software segment, its evolution, complexities, trends and possible future. It should prove to be an invaluable tool for anyone who is faced with planning a selection exercise or who is planning to work for an ETRM vendor or services provider.

The book also contains articles by its sponsors, Allegro Development and SAS RiskAvisory. UtiliPoint appreciates their support of this project and believes that their articles add significant value to its content.

Dr. Gary M. Vasey   Andrew Bruce
VP, Macroenergy Analysis   VP, Trading & Risk Management Practice
UtiliPoint International, Inc.   UtiliPoint International, Inc.

Houston, TX
February, 2006

ONE

WHAT IS ENERGY TRADING, TRANSACTION AND RISK MANAGEMENT SOFTWARE?

Dr. Gary M. Vasey,
UtiliPoint International, Inc.

Energy trading, transaction and risk management (ETRM) software is that category of software applications, architectures and tools that supports the business processes associated with energy trading. In this sense, energy trading means the buying and selling of energy commodities such as crude oil, coal, natural gas, electric power and refined products, the management of the movement and delivery of the energy commodities and associated risk management activities. ETRM software comprises a broad set of functions that can vary considerably depending on what commodities are traded, what assets are employed in the business, where those assets are located, and what the company's business strategy and associated business processes are. Today, the impact of regulations such as the Sarbanes-Oxley Act and recommendations from the Committee of Chief Risk Officers, amongst others are having a further impact on the requirements for ETRM software.

Usually and in the broadest sense, ETRM solutions are fully integrated sets of software that help to manage the front, middle and back office aspects of an energy trading entity. Although definitions and organizational structures differ quite widely, the front office is usually concerned with deal capture and position management, the middle office with managing and reporting various risk exposures as a result of trading activities and the back office with settlements and accounting functions. Additionally, there will usually be a scheduling component to ETRM solutions allowing the energy company to plan, track, manage and account for quantities of energy that have to be physically moved from source to point of usage.

Although ETRM software functional coverage can be difficult to define, another way to look at it is to consider the types of company that need to utilize ETRM software as follows:-

• Hedge Funds trading energy commodities
• Investment banks trading commodities

- Energy merchants trading commodities
- Multinational oil companies trading commodities
- Producers selling their production
- Utilities (Investor-owned, Municipal utilities and cooperatives) buying fuel for power generation and for the sale of wholesale gas or electric power
- Local Distribution Companies buying wholesale energy to sell to retail markets
- Large commercial and industrial end users of energy
- Petrochemical and refining companies that procure feedstock in wholesale markets

Given the list of different segments of the energy industry that might require it to use ETRM software, it can be readily understood that the required functionality of such systems can be extensive. Another way to think about ETRM software is to consider the management of two primary functions across these entities. First is the business of managing the assets employed in the business whether those assets are generation facilities, produced quantities of oil, gas or electric power, and secondly the merchant function that is involved in the buying and selling of commodities and managing the associated risks. ETRM software is used to manage the merchant function and has to be fully integrated with the asset management function.

It is actually very difficult to define the entire functional coverage of an ETRM system simply as a result of the different variations in requirements at the detailed level. However, on a broad level, the software will comprise most of the following applications or functions;

Front Office Applications

Electronic Trading

The heyday of electronic trading came to an abrupt end along with the collapse of the mega-merchant segment of the industry. Prior to the aftermath of Enron, online energy trading had grown at an incredibly fast rate. In 2000, $400 billion was actively traded online, a 750 percent jump from the year before. The last several years have seen electronic transactions decrease until recently when the return of speculators to the market (hedge funds, investment banks, proprietary trading desks) began a recovery.

The resurgence in electronic trading has benefited those that survived including Intercontinental exchange (ICE) and one or two others. However, electronic trading is utilized by a variety of industry players that conduct trades and those trades need to be captured in the ETRM system so as to insure that it is the primary system for position keeping and risk management.

Deal Capture

The deal capture application area supports the traders and/or administrators capture of deals into the system for further processing. Generally, deal capture is the start of the transaction flow through to invoicing but it usually requires other set up data to function correctly such as contract and counterparty data. Deal capture requires a high level of ease of use to allow traders and administrators to enter deals rapidly. Many vendors have therefore developed "deal blotter" screens in addition to long-form deal capture screens. The deal blotter screen looks and behaves like a spreadsheet and is a familiar environment for traders. Additionally, it may often be configured for a specific trader allowing the trader to default many of the data items on the screen for more rapid data capture.

Deal capture systems are required to be able to capture any number of transactions both physical and financial. It is this that adds to the complexity of deal capture systems since each deal type requires any number of additional and unique attributes to be entered. One issue that may arise with the deal capture function is in capturing physical and financial deals in different systems. Financial deals may sometimes be captured in a risk system while the physical deals are captured in the transaction management systems. This results in a need to link corresponding deals and can lead to integration and position keeping problems.

As the industry has evolved, the deal capture business function has become more standardized, with better definition of instruments and deal types across the industry. In turn, this has allowed vendors and solution providers to develop better solutions to support traders. Nonetheless, deal capture can be a complex piece of functionality especially if it is combined with trader tools for what-if analysis and if it is required to provide instantaneous valuation and risk measures such as Value at Risk and Mark to Market valuation.

Despite the increased standardization in this business function, since it is often provided as a module in a broader-based solution, it is rarely deployed as a stand-alone solution. In almost all cases, the deal capture module is bundled with other functionality to provide transaction processing through pre-scheduling and often to invoice.

There are many ways in which deals get done today including over the telephone, through an exchange, using Interactive Messaging and email. All of these different media have to be captured in the ETRM's deal capture area.

Real-time Trade Capture

For any power company with generation, real-time trading also has to be performed and those deals captured in the system. Real-time trading is conducted to maintain balance as generation operations progress and as real-time needs arise on the grid and is a separate function from the actual wholesale trading operations that deal with time periods beyond the day of operations. Real-time trading is therefore more typically a requirement for utilities and generators than merchants and often managed by the regulated arm of the company.

Trader Analytics

Analytic tools to support traders in their activities have become common additions to many ETRM systems in recent years. These tools can include price calculators (option prices, etc.) as well as "what-if" tools allowing traders to analyze the impact of a trade against a portfolio. One evolution that has taken place in the analytics area is one from models developed primarily for financial markets to more energy-specific models that take account of the specific behavior of the underlying commodity.

Position Keeping

Position keeping is the function that essentially tracks trades and their offsetting physical and financial positions and has long been an area of short coming in many trading/marketing departments and systems. Despite the fact that most third-party packages provide some position keeping functionality, many trading floors still rely on manually update whiteboards and spreadsheets to keep overall position. The issue is partly about the diversity of systems used by marketers/traders and the lack of a coherent integration framework that can bring all the required data together and present it in a usable form and, partly related to business process shortcomings – particularly where deals are entered after the fact. Position is required in multiple formats. For example, overall portfolio position, position at various points on the grid as well as physical and financial position. It is this level of complexity that has kept position keeping a largely manual activity in many marketing/trading shops.

Scheduling Applications

Pre-Scheduling and Scheduling

Scheduling involves organizing the movement of physical energy commodity via some transport mechanism and for that reason scheduling systems have different functionality depending upon the commodity to be scheduled and the geographic location in which the movement will take place. Scheduling or pre-scheduling is another function that can be extremely complex and that many vendor-provided solutions still fail to address completely. In North America, gas scheduling comprises pathing, nominating and confirming gas volumes through various pipelines whereas electric power scheduling involves pathing power through various grids and communicating back and forth with the regional power markets. Scheduling for other commodities such as crude oil and coal may involve utilizing barges, trains, trucks or vessels and the tracking of those shipments from one place to another.

Scheduling is a function that both plans the movement of the commodity but also tracks and accounts for that movement. So for example, a company may plan to move a volume of natural gas along a pipeline but it needs to have the legal right to do so and then communicate back and forth with the pipeline on issues such as the actual volumes delivered and shipped, the transportation costs and any losses in volume that take place on the pipeline and so on. It is a very complex function and different solutions are required for each commodity and geography.

eTagging & ISO/RTO Interfacing

These functions are important in scheduling electric power in North America and as the interfacing and e-tagging requirements are largely regional (by ISO or RTO) in nature, this business function has not and might never truly standardize in North America. It therefore provides a niche opportunity for specialist solution providers. The function involves communicating to the regional power market operator using its standards for data interchange as well as reconciling and settling on the actual quantities that moved.

Middle Office Applications

Risk Management

Risk management systems in the energy industry became essential tools after wholesale power markets opened up. The instantaneous nature of power, its lack of storage capabilities and price volatility drove the adoption of risk management across the industry. The risk system generally captures financial trades directly and then provides various exposure reports for both financial and physical trades/portfolios. Many risk systems provide a variety of tools to value trades, books and portfolios including Value at Risk and Earnings at Risk. The diversity of instruments/trades that need to be represented in risk systems may include weather, interest rates and foreign exchange transactions as well as energy commodity related instruments. Risk system vendors are now adding methods and reports to address aspects of the physical side of the business such as volumetric risk. Earnings at Risk and similar tools are an example of the shift that has taken place in this area. Earnings at Risk possibly provides a better assessment of how earnings would be impacted by certain events or price movements as opposed to making the assumption that positions can be unwound. For marketers with generation, for example, power is actually taken to delivery and therefore the position cannot be "unwound" in the same way that a financial position might be. This volumetric risk aspect to today's power marketers' business differs considerably to the market risks faced by asset-light merchants.

Another facet of the changing risk management world is the mark-to-market valuation versus accrual accounting often used by utilities. While mark-to-market valuation is a common and accepted method, the difficulty is in understanding how a mark-to-market profit actually gets booked on an accrual basis. Often, traders and marketers have been rewarded based on mark-to-market position as opposed to actual accrued profits. In the past, price manipulation resulted in inflated mark-to-market valuations that after settlement weren't reflected in the company's books, causing apparent profits to "evaporate." As a result, more emphasis is now placed on independent price data but this is difficult in more opaque Over the Counter (OTC) transactions.

Credit Management

Credit management and credit risk management has become an area of concern for all energy companies after the collapse of the merchants and the counterparty credit issues that followed. The credit management function requires access to contract data as well as external credit agency and other credit data. The credit function usually establishes credit profiles for counterparties, monitors credit limits against counterparties as well as manages collateral requirements. It has rapidly become something of a specialized function that has growing importance and is now served by specific credit management application providers.

Additionally, many of the existing ETRM platform vendors also provide some credit management functionality. In this instance, the functionality is usually limited to monitoring trade exposure to counterparties although some systems do go further. Very few traditional trading and transaction management systems however also manage the collateral side of credit management.

With the ongoing emphasis on credit and collateral management as a component of good corporate governance and risk management, this is an area that may see a continued emergence of specialist vendors and a requirement to integrate with existing trading and transaction management systems.

For marketers with both wholesale and retail operations, credit management is a much more complex proposition. If utilizing an ETRM system's credit functionality, this is generally built to provide credit management for wholesale trading activities only lacking the ability and scalability to manage counterparty credit exposure for thousands of retail counterparties. Generally, the solution is to aggregate like contracts into groups and then load those into the credit management module and this again requires external spreadsheets or customized solutions be built.

Additionally, there are developing a number of risk measures such as Credit Value at Risk (CVaR). While some systems ostensibly offer the ability to calculate and report on CVaR, the devil is in the details of the methodology and the ability to enter and store credit data at the appropriate level.

Back Office Applications

Contract Management

Contract Management data is a key component for trading, credit management and scheduling activities and it is generally provided as a part of an ETRM system. Generally, these systems maintain the key contract data that provides for counterparty credit limit monitoring, transmission terms and trading limits, and so on.

Settlement & Invoicing

While settlement and invoicing are often grouped together, they are two different and important functions. While both functions are often provided by ETRM software packages, many companies actually utilize solutions other than their primary ETRM system to perform these functions. Again, while invoicing is a function provided by many of the primary trading and transaction management systems, but many companies also utilize a different system to produce invoices.

Hedge Accounting

Hedge Accounting has become a mandatory function since the inception of FAS 133 and its equivalent accounting standards. As with credit management, a host of niche solutions has been developed specifically to help perform hedge accounting. At the same time, many traditional vendors have added some degree of hedge accounting functionality to their systems, too.

Other ETRM Functions

Depending upon the type of company utilizing and ETRM system a number of other functions may be required including gas storage, inventory management, generation dispatch, load forecasting, market simulation, stress testing, gas measurement, and more. Additionally, all ETRM solutions will require some administrative functions including security of access, audit trailing, workflow, interfaces to external price feeds and other external data sources and, document management.

Part of the complexity of ETRM is that there is no standard for what comprises an ETRM system. However, as regulations and recommendations are made by various organizations and governing bodies, more standardized approaches are emerging in areas such as risk management, deal capture, and the back office. Still, as the ETRM software class serves such a broad set of essentially niche markets from hedge funds to regional utilities, what constitutes an ETRM solution is very variable. It is this that allows so many vendors and products to coexist in the industry since many products are targeted at niche vertical markets or at specific functions within the context of ETRM.

Some ETRM software solutions have gone further in terms of back office functionality too and offer general ledger, accounts payable and accounts receivable functions. However, many energy companies utilize their existing accounting packages to perform much of this functionality requiring an interface between the ETRM system and the accounting system.

The energy industry is actually a very heterogeneous market for ETRM software with horizontal and vertical niches that, on the surface at least, appear to share similar requirements. While many "outsiders" see a large and attractive homogeneous market for ETRM software with good revenue and profit potential, the truth is that there are a plethora of energy company business models and each model has its own detailed version of the same set of requirements. Indeed, at a certain level of detail, all energy companies involved in buying and selling energy commodities have common business functions yet, as you drill down, there are significant and fundamental differences in those requirements. The idea that there are standard function-ality requirements is simply a mirage created by a fundamental lack of understanding of the energy business at a detailed level.

Requirements Dictated By Assets and Location

The nature of each energy company's physical assets and the geographic location of those assets actually dictate the majority of the software requirements at the detailed level. The need to record and report on data and transactions is inevitably governed by the regulatory regimes under which the company operates its assets and by the type of assets employed in the business. For example, an electric generator with predominately hydro generation facilities will have different requirements from the company that has predominantly coal-fired facilities. Generators in different geographic regions will have different reporting requirements. During the energy trading bubble, the fundamental importance of assets was overlooked and the recent return to asset-centric trading has increased the importance of asset-related software requirements.

Traditional Software Business Model

Energy software vendors largely follow a traditional packaged software business model that requires them to sell more and more software licenses. The presumption behind this model is that a single shrink-wrapped packaged software application has a large enough potential market to support it. The truth is that, in the energy industry, this is often simply not the case.

Vendor's products tend to evolve into increasingly complex software as they are sold into an ever-larger installed base simply because the vendor has to enhance and modify its software to meet the specific requirements of each new additional customer. The end result is often a near unsupport-able set of spaghetti code. Worse still, in the hands of a poorly capitalized vendor, the problem is further magnified, as the vendor has insufficient cash to keep up the support and ongoing enhancement of the product that is needed to pursue the traditional software business model.

There are two fundamental reasons for this state of affairs. First, this is not a traditional shrink-wrap software package market and second, the industry has not yet evolved to a point of sufficient stability to support a traditional software model. Indeed, the history of this software category demonstrates both these assertions admirably.

No Emergence of Mega Vendors?

In spite of the history of the industry and its inherent volatility, anyone looking for ETRM software today without the benefit of hindsight could be forgiven for believing that two to three mega vendors may have emerged. While it is certainly true that there are two or three more dominant vendors, one needs to look at the products, not the vendors. At that point one discovers that the dominance came through the acquisition of stranded vendors and products. In other words, the vendor has multiple product platforms, many nearing end of life, few of which are likely well suited to today's energy company looking for a product. That is not to say that these vendors' products are not suited to some energy companies. It's just that there is no single dominant product in the market.

While the energy industry continues to evolve with periods of tremendous demand for software followed by periods of uncertainty and change, no dominant product or vendor can emerge, especially if a traditional package software model is pursued by the vendor. But why do vendors adopt the traditional package model if it doesn't work? The answer lies in both the economies of scale that can benefit the buyers of packaged software and also in the vendors' need for outside venture capital. Obtaining outside investment is often difficult if an unusual business model is adopted by the vendor and valuations are considered higher for vendors with a high software license revenue component.

Integration and the Search for the Solution

To be fair to the vendors, many have recognized the significant issues facing them. Buyers too, especially the more savvy variety who have had some experience in the software market, recognized that it was unlikely there would be a single supplier of the complete solution. Both buyer and vendor eyed a "best of breed" model where software could be written to perform a particular set of business functions extremely well. For example, energy risk management or scheduling applications could be developed as best of breed applications.

However, in a best of breed architecture a new problem emerges. How to integrate the best of breed applications to build a seamless solution for the entire trading operation? The answer was to deploy middleware. While buyers sought to find suitable suppliers of middleware, many vendors tried to build middleware into their own application suites thus creating a complete single source solution comprised of best of breed components.

At this point, the experience in the industry has been that the introduction of middleware increases project complexity, risks and costs to an unacceptable level for all but the largest of energy firms. It is simply very difficult to achieve a complete set of integrated applications in a business environment that is still so dynamic. For example, as each vendor attempts to keep up with industry requirements for their best of breed applications, they are forced to issue several upgrades each year. This presents a considerable problem for the buyer who is either faced with falling behind on their vendor's software and of course, new functionality that might be imperative, or continually revisiting the integration framework as they "bolt in" the upgrades. Those searching for a complete set of integrated and customizable software applications have until recently been disappointed.

If it's Not a Package Market - Then What is It?

To be successful, the vendors have to adopt different business models that essentially allow them to escape the endless cycles of market growth and dislocation. Not only would this provide the industry with vendor and product stability, it might also lead to the emergence of stable, long-lasting vendors that offer what the industry really needs in terms of its software requirements.

There are new business models developing that might provide the answers. They range from the use of new software architectures and tools that incorporate the connectivity such as Web services to models that implicitly recognize the limitations of the traditional packaged software business model.

Summary

It is difficult to define ETRM software precisely. At its core, ETRM software comprises deal capture, position keeping, risk management, settlement and invoicing along with some scheduling modules organized such that data is entered only once and flows through the system from the front office to the back office. In reality, each company using an ETRM solution has its own particular requirements and each vertical market niche from production to local distribution requires some variation in functionality and some extensions to functionality.

TWO

THE HISTORY OF ETRM SOFTWARE PRODUCTS AND VENDORS

By Dr. Gary M. Vasey,
UtiliPoint International, Inc.

The ETRM software space has evolved rapidly in step with the industry and its requirements, and it is important that this evolution and hence, some of the historical issues, are understood. Since FERC Order 636 effectively created the ETRM software category just 13 or so years ago, ETRM software vendors and products alike have arrived and then disappeared again in response to the volatility of the energy trading industry. This section outlines the history of the software category against the background of industry events and provides insights into how the different vendors and products have evolved over this time.

Pre-FERC Order 636

Before the onset of wholesale trading in natural gas was enabled by FERC Order 636 and subsequent orders, natural gas marketing software functionality had been a "module" in the production and revenue accounting systems used by producers to account for the volumes, revenues, and disbursements associated with their natural gas marketing operations. Most of the major production & revenue management systems were large-scale, mainframe-based systems available from accounting and consulting firms such as Andersen Consulting and Price Waterhouse or, for the middle tier of the market, midrange solutions on AS 400's or similar, from a variety of smaller software vendors. Some of those smaller vendors included extant energy software companies such as Allegro Development, Energy Solutions, and Ensyte Energy Software.

FERC 636 resulted in the creation of wholesale markets for natural gas and the gas marketing firms that played them thereby creating a need for a new and specific solution – the natural gas marketing system.

The Natural Gas Marketing Explosion

The effects of FERC Order 636 in 1992 also coincided fortuitously with the emergence of client/server technology and architectures as a low cost, scalable, and fairly powerful computing platform. More importantly, the client/server revolution was initially led by California-based database maker Sybase, Inc. Until that point, the energy and utility industry had been dominated by Oracle but the emergence of a new need for natural gas marketing systems allowed Sybase a beachhead in the industry by virtue of its innovation of the client/server model complete with database "triggers".

Initially, the sizeable "virgin" market for gas marketing systems resulted in many marketers electing to build their own systems, often choosing Sybase as the platform of choice. At the same time, a number of software entrepreneurs also saw the opportunity that FERC Order 636 presented, often as a result of being contracted to help build a gas marketing solution, or by being involved with an in-house development. Similarly, some of the peripheral mid-range platform production and revenue management software vendors saw the potential offered by FERC 636 and the industry change that followed, and they too looked for opportunities to build gas marketing systems.

Although most of the emphasis was naturally upon the physical side of the natural gas marketing business, developing systems to capture and maintain contracts, "trades", position, and schedule the gas to a variety of different pipelines, one or two early vendors also focused on the risk management side of natural gas marketing (See Table 2.1). Many systems were also designed to provide accounting support for natural gas marketing activities including accruals, AR, AP, and even GL support. However, the emphasis lay naturally on nomination and confirmation to pipelines and in capturing contracts and trades. Despite work by the Gas Industry Standards Board (GISB), data interchange with pipelines has remained fairly pipeline-specific in North America, meaning that much of the complexity of these systems was to be found in their scheduling functionality.

All of the original vendors of gas marketing software can be character-ized as small, cash-strapped start-ups or small existing private software firms. Most relied heavily on an early client to help define the software's business requirements, and/or to support the initial development of their software. Many made good initial progress in licensing their software to a small number of the firms marketing gas.

Typically, in this new and rapidly evolving software market, the gas marketing firms decided to build and deploy home-grown systems rather than rely on the offerings of a group of small and unstable vendors. Tenneco utilized its own platform, as did Williams, PanEnergy, and Aquila, among others. In some instances the energy company also attempted to market its own internally developed software to other gas marketers. For a while, Tenneco marketed its' system under the "EnergyTracs" brand, Aquila's software was marketed through a third-party and was known as "RiskWorks," while the Williams and PanEnergy efforts were eventually combined to form Altra Energy Technologies in January 1996. Ultimately, these energy company software ventures were deemed by their owners to be "non-core" businesses and either ended up in the hands of true commercial vendors (e.g. SunGard acquired RiskWorks and TransEnergy acquired the source code for EnergyTracs), or in software companies specifically created for the purpose of taking the software to market (e.g. Altra Energy).

Early commercially available software solutions were usually incomplete, often "buggy," of suspicious initial software quality levels, and were typically licensed by "early adopter" purchasers who were willing to tolerate such issues. As software was sold by the vendors to new accounts, it also required fairly substantial enhancement and modifications. Nonetheless, the early software vendors competed enthusiastically for new business and the segment started to mature. Because of the complexity of the physical business, a system seeded at one gas marketing entity was often only a partial fit for other gas marketers, resulting in a rapid evolution of the software products.

Table 2.1 A Selection of Early Natural Gas Marketing Vendors

New Entrants

- TransGas Management (renamed TransEnergy Management later – founded 1988)
- Altra Energy Technologies (Williams & PanEnergy founded December 1995/January 1996)
- Tenneco (TenSpeed System later marketed as Energy TRACS – around 1994/5)
- Data Management Solutions (founded 1993)
- DC Systems, Inc. (founded 1989)
- Primo, Inc. (founded 1992-1993)
- Aquila – RiskWorks (built prior to 1996)

Survivors

- Allegro Development Corporation (founded 1984)
- Energy Solutions, Inc. (founded 1983 as micro solutions)
- Michael Smith & Associates (Ensyte Energy Software – founded 1982);

Note: Survivors emerged from the mid-range production & revenue accounting world.

Power Markets Follow

Even as the gas marketing software vendors were establishing themselves, another round of deregulation was already being discussed that would disrupt this emerging software market – electric power. The deregulation of wholesale power markets in North America under FERC Order 888 of 1996 had a number of impacts:

- Power, being instantaneous, could not be effectively stored creating an immediate requirement for better risk management tools;
- Many fledging marketers and energy firms began to consider also entering the power markets;

It was the latter fact, in particular, that would have far reaching consequences on the fledgling gas marketing software markets, delaying software procurement decisions while energy companies re-established their business strategies. In fact, the deregulation of electric power created an elongated period of uncertainty and a major "dislocation" event.

Dislocation Events in Software Markets

UtiliPoint's market dislocation model adopts the hypothesis that a market for any new software product ought to follow a classical technology adoption curve with early adopters nurturing early vendors and products into maturity, and a majority of buyers later adopting the resulting standard software. Early adopters take a bet on a certain vendor/product and work with the technology until it either fails to evolve at all or, both the product and the market for the product matures sufficiently for there to be sustaining demand. Early vendors in any market are usually bootstrapped or venture capital-backed start-ups with visionary leaders who see a market.

Figure 2.1: Technology Adoption Curve

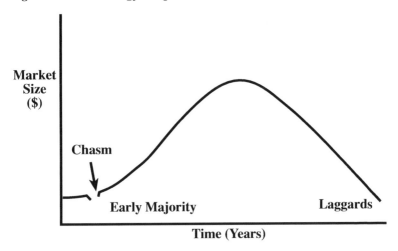

If the technology adoption curve is disrupted or dislocated by subsequent market changes, then usually the market simply dissolves and its vendors and products disappear – there being no market. However, in the case of ETRM software, while the technology adoption curve was certainly truncated, after a period of uncertainty, a changed, but potentially even larger market was created. The original market did not die but was simply diminished in size and growth potential while a new and changed market evolved creating a new and larger adoption curve.

The change in business requirements was never sufficient to kill off the ETRM category altogether but each industry change had a dramatic impact on the vendors and products in the market. As Figure 2.2 shows, the results of each dislocation event can be categorized as follows:

• *Stranded Vendors* – Poorly capitalized or over-stretched vendors unable to follow the change in the market are essentially "stranded" as niche vendors following the original "stunted" market;

• *Survivors* – Vendors able to evolve their software products fast enough to meet the needs of the new market are able to survive the event and carry on;

• *New Entrants* – The dislocation event has two characteristics, a delay in adoption during a period of uncertainty and the emergence of a new and possibly even more attractive market. As a result, each dislocation event creates an opportunity for new entrants, either from software markets peripheral to the ETRM software market, or through new start-ups. A further characteristic of the new entrant is the ability to acquire the stranded vendors and products as a way to enter the market with an installed base.

Figure 2.2 a-cMorphology of a dislocation event

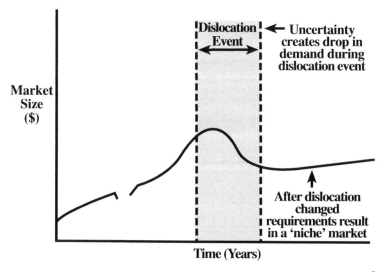

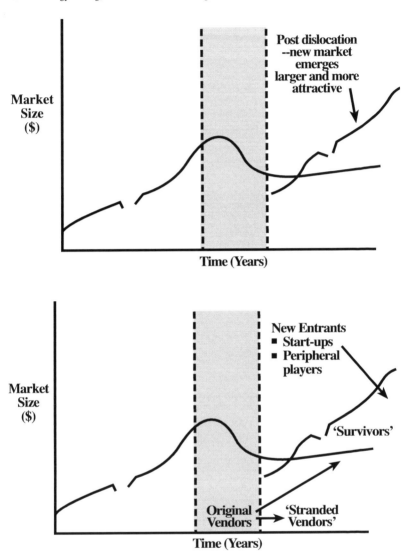

The Impact of the Deregulation of Electric Power

The advent of wholesale power markets and trading brought with it the concepts of trading multiple energy commodities and also of risk management. The period of uncertainty associated with this event resulted in many months of reduced demand for gas marketing software vendor's software since many marketers were considering becoming power marketers too and they needed to re-evaluate both their business strategy and systems requirements. For example, TransGas Management went for eight or nine months without a new license sale during this period and, had it not been for timely venture capital funding, may not have survived the dislocation event at all.

The new ETRM software market that finally emerged after this period of uncertainty was both larger and more attractive than the relatively small gas marketing software market and thus, it attracted many new entrants. Specifically, there were two types of new entrants at that time:

1. Larger software, services and, other firms from peripheral markets including the financial and banking segment (e.g. Zai*Net Software, OpenLink Financial, SunGard), true EMS vendors from the generation and controls world (ABB for example), and software companies targeting specific niches in the utilities and generation world (Henwood, New Energy Associates, for example);

2. Start-ups that emerged either as a small team of entrepreneurial developers such as Nucleus and ArcIT, or as consultants building a custom solution that was subsequently marketed (PowerTrade, for example).

Among the existing gas marketing software vendors, some fell behind as stranded vendors to remain focused on the smaller natural gas marketing software markets, such as DC Systems, Energy Solutions, and Ensyte Energy Software, while others that either had taken in venture capital, or who had supporting customers, were able to survive, at least for a time, as multi-commodity platform and risk management vendors. These includes Altra, TransEnergy (which changed its name from TransGas Management to TransEnergy Management to emphasize this fact), and Allegro Development (See Table 2.2.).

Some of the newly entering software companies did so through the acquisition of stranded vendors and their installed base. For example, SunGard initially entered the market by acquiring Primo Systems. Others saw the potential for peripheral software products in wholesale power markets (e.g. ABB, New Energy Associates and, Henwood).

Nucleus, PowerTrade, EnerX Development and, ArcIT all got started around this time developing systems at specific customer sites and, after delivery, started to market their software products more broadly. Interestingly, Zai*Net Software actually commenced life as a risk system for FX transactions but, seeing the power markets open up, rapidly moved into energy markets to exploit it – even notifying existing clients of its decision.

Table 2.2 Vendors in the gas and power trading, transaction and risk management market

Survivors:	TransGas Management as
	TransEnergy Management
	Altra Energy
	Allegro Development
Stranded Vendors:	DC Systems
	ESI
	Ensyte Energy Software
	DMS
	Primo Systems
	Energy TRACS
	RiskWorks
New Entrants:	Zai*Net Software
	SunGard
	OpenLink Financial
	ABB
	Henwood
	New Energy Associates
	PowerTrade
	ArcIT
	EnerX Development
	Nucleus
	ACES

For survivors, this was a time of challenge since the initial inclination was to modify their gas marketing systems to be power marketing systems. However, early on, this approach was deemed to be a failure owing to the dynamic nature of electric power; the complexity of the scheduling process, including book outs and daisy chains; as well as the fact that, while gas was monthly and daily, electric power was daily and hourly, and the system had to account for the complexities of off-peak, on-peak and NERC holidays.

Additionally, almost immediately, marketers began to also demand price risk management tools and so the survivors needed to build, not just power marketing software, but risk management software as well. The answer was to find a sponsoring customer or group of customers who would fund the subsequent development of these products and TransEnergy, Altra, and Allegro, all in time, announced risk systems and electric power transaction management systems as a result of this type of initiative. It was the emerging risk element that also attracted financial risk management vendors such as OpenLink Financial and Zai*Net Software into the fray. Built and designed to cater to financial trading with various forms of derivative instruments and then to calculate mark-to-market, value at risk and, other risk measures using forward price curves, OpenLink and Zai*Net were able to enter the market as energy risk systems. However, both vendors lacked any semblance of physical transaction management capabilities initially for any physical energy commodity.

In effect, immediately after FERC Order 888, the market was still immature, confused, and filled with competing vendors all with incomplete products. As a result, other ventures such as Henwood, New Energy Associates and, ABB were also able to build software products for customers peripheral to their existing software offerings while consultants were able to build and deploy custom solutions, some of which (Nucleus, PowerTrade, EnerX, and Arc IT, for example) attempted to re-sell them as software packages. Meanwhile, the stranded gas marketing vendors remained focused on selling their software to marketing companies, producers, LDCs and, other companies that remained focused on natural gas.

Multi-commodity trading, transaction and risk management

Shortly after the emergence of wholesale power trading and the rapid rise of the merchants led by Enron, Dynegy, and others, the requirement for software began to take on another new dimension. What was now required was software systems capable of supporting both physical and financial trading with straight through processing capabilities for multiple energy and energy-related commodities. This need provided opportunities for other vendors to enter the market and play a role. In existence for some time, vendors such as SolArc, with products targeting crude oil and

NGL marketing, and Triple Point Technologies, with a similar product mix, began to gain in recognition along with the power and gas vendors. Triple Point in particular embarked on building gas and power marketing solutions to round out its product suite.

While the existing vendors struggled somewhat to attain this new goal, some using acquisitions to accelerate their abilities, middleware came to be seen as a potential solution. The hope was, that by using middleware such as that provided by TibCo, Vitria, Knowmadic and others, many of these competing software products could be "bolted" together to provide a best-of-breed solution. However, outside of some of the larger merchants, the middleware approach often proved to be both too costly and too complex to bear real fruit – but it took several years to find that out.

During this period, vendors understood that customers were looking for complete end-to-end solutions with complete commodity coverage. Unfortunately, the vendors were often too small to be able to afford the necessary product investment required to produce such a solution. While many vendors teamed up with middleware providers in an attempt to build in a messaging framework that would allow the software products to be connected seamlessly, they were also dealing with growing installed bases and ever-broadening product suites. The net result of this set of challenges was for vendors to over reach themselves marketing both functions and features that were planned but not necessarily present in the software and, attempting to support large amounts of code across a very diverse installed base. With multiple market niches (producers, LDCs, generators, utilities of various types, merchants, etc.) to target and a need for a constant supply of cash from new software licenses, many vendors targeted multiple market niches simultaneously trying to satisfy the diverse requirements of each within a single software product or suite of products. Each new customer had truly unique requirements and therefore each required further enhancements. As a result, product strategies became dictated by the need to sign new customers as opposed to ensuring that existing customers' needs were truly met.

When combined with the small size and relative immaturity of the vendor's own internal organizations, there were a number of issues that had a serious impact on the evolution of this software category:

• Software quality – growing code lines and a shortage of internal product knowledgeable resources often resulted in unsatisfactory software quality. Bug fixing became more and more difficult since a fix in one part of the product would often break another part of the software. Lacking the resources, internal methods and, tools to properly test the software, initial quality declined;

- The pace of change in the industry combined with the need to deliver enhancements and bug fixes resulted in difficult to manage release plans. Vendors were often forced to release software upgrades on a monthly basis. Since the quality of the software was suspect, many users simply did not keep up with this rapid pace of software upgrade releases, becoming left behind on older versions of the vendor's software;

- The rapid growth of many of the software companies caused real growth pains that were reflected in the inability to properly train new hires on the industry and the products. This impacted all aspects of the vendor's ability to deliver but it also meant that many placed raw recruits on important implementation projects. Consequently, products were often poorly implemented and poorly configured to meet the needs of the customer;

- This growth challenge also resulted in a "brain trust" where just a few resources really understood the product. Once a customer had exposure to one of these key resources that customer only ever wanted to have access to that resource, circumventing any attempts by the vendor to build a proper support organization. Similarly, every internal product development decision made by the vendor required the brain trust to be involved. Naturally, the brain trust was overworked and spread too thin.

There were other issues impacting the vendor's ability to deliver in addition to those above, ranging from over-selling and over-marketing to staff burnout issues. One consequence of this was that vendors and products began to be replaced by customers in the search for a better solution and better service. Indeed, buyers became disillusioned with the software category altogether and began to seek alternative suppliers.

Meanwhile, there was another trend at play in the industry – globalization. As deregulation (or liberalization) was introduced into other parts of the world, including most of Europe, there was some attempt by merchants and utilities to grow in other regions through acquisition. European companies acquired North American assets and vice versa. Accompanying this trend was the globalization of the vendors. Companies such as Altra, TransEnergy, Caminus, OpenLink and, others entered Europe while existing European vendors such as KWI, Vedaris (formerly FSD International) and, Murex moved into North America with varying degrees of success. Part of that success was based on the buyer's perception that these European vendors had a fresh offering for North American markets.

The Implications of North American Retail Deregulation

Retail deregulation held high hopes but given the California experience, it has largely failed to materialize in North America. A number of states have moved forward with retail deregulation plans but the effort has not occurred on the scale imagined earlier. Despite that, retail deregulation attracted the attention of a number of the vendors in the space with a rush to develop or modify software to cater for the coming retail markets. For most, the effort to respond to this market opportunity, coming as it did on the back of some of the other opportunities, was simply too much. However, other vendors were attracted by the opportunity, including Excelergy and New Energy Associates, for example.

Table 2.3 Example list of vendors prior to the merchant collapse

Survivors:	SunGard Energy Systems
	Caminus
	Allegro Development
	OLF
	Triple Point
	SoftSmiths
	Henwood
	NEA
	Structure Group
	eAcumen
Stranded Vendors:	DMS
	ESI
	Ensyte
	Energy Softworx
	ABB
	PowerTrade
New Entrants:	Kiodex
	KWI
	Vedaris
	Algorithmics
	OATI
	Alstom ESCA
	SAS
	Excelergy
	OM Technologies
	Woodlands Technologies

The Collapse of the Mega-Merchant

Looking back, it was only natural that something 'big' would happen to this rapidly growing, highly competitive and immature software market and it did. The downfall of Enron, rapidly followed by the other mega-merchants, and retrenchment of utilities back to a safer business model created another extended period of uncertainty and a dislocation event that would help narrow the field while once again providing an opportunity for new vendors to enter. Perhaps the most significant dislocation event to date, the period of uncertainty lasted three years and has only recently come to an end.

This dislocation event had a tremendous impact on the vendors. Several vendors failed following the demise of the merchant sector, among them eAcumen and Vedaris. Sales cycles were stretched out for an extended period of time causing significant cash flow problems for all vendors. Several significant acquisitions also took place during this period, including SunGard's acquisition of Caminus, Barra's acquisition of FEA, and the funding/acquisition of vendors such as Henwood, ABB's software and KWI by Global Energy Decisions, LLC (which also acquired eAcumen's power product), and of New Energy Associates by Siemens. Additionally, there were several "new entrants" including the aforementioned Global Energy Decisions, but also vendors such as Woodland Technologies, which brought new products to market during the period of uncertainty and was itself acquired by New Energy Associates. Additionally, The Structure Group purchased the assets of PowerTrade.

The market for ETRM software is now rebounding as energy companies determine their strategies for the future and as investment banks, hedge funds and other entities enter the energy trading space. However, the industry's requirements continue to change and morph such that there remain over 65 vendors and solutions active in the ETRM space today and new vendors continue to emerge.

Table 2.4 – Summary of vendors after the Merchant Collapse

Survivors:	SunGard Energy Systems
	Kiodex
	Allegro Development
	OLF
	Algorithmics
	Triple Point
	OATI
	SoftSmiths
	SAS
	Structure Group
	Excelergy
Stranded Vendors:	DMS
	ESI
	Ensyte
	Energy Softworx
	PowerTrade
New Entrants:	Global Energy Decisions
	Siemens
	E-Systems
	TrinityApex

THREE

THE CURRENT STATUS OF ETRM SOFTWARE

By Dr. Gary M. Vasey, Christopher Perdue,
UtiliPoint International and Kevin Rose, EnSight Advisors

The current status of ETRM software can probably be judged as falling into two distinct groups – the installed solutions actually used by firms that trade energy and, the current vendor software offerings. Often, these are two different things since:

• Many installed vendor solutions have fallen behind the vendor's current version due to upgrade issues and the pace of industry changes;

• Many installed vendor products are no longer truly supported or are likely to become unsupported in future years as a result of merger and acquisition activities between vendors; and,

• There has been a migration of software architecture over the last 24 months that is still in progress away from client/server technology to n-tier, componentized architectures.

    This section will focus in on the former group being the software actually installed at user sites across North America and will use two ground breaking studies by UtiliPoint on ETRM software conducted in 2004 and 2005 in electric power and natural gas respectively[1] . These two studies were comprehensive reviews of the installed software used to support electricity trading, transaction and risk management and in the natural gas side of the industry. In total some 38 companies participated in the electric power study and 28 companies in the natural gas study representing a fair cross section of North American energy companies. If the studies had a weakness, it would be that the respondents were skewed towards smaller energy companies in general. The two studies are available from UtiliPoint.

    While many of the study respondents utilized third-party vendor software, the surveys clearly demonstrated that many solutions for different areas of the energy trading business are still internally developed or served by spreadsheets. Generally, the survey respondents indicated that they were

---

[1]Evaluation and Benchmarking of Natural Gas Software Application Usage in North American Gas Companies, 2005 and Evaluation and Benchmark of Information Technology at North American Power Marketing Organizations, 2004. UtiliPoint International.

satisfied with the ETRM software solutions deployed to support wholesale trading and risk management activities (whether vendor-provided, internally developed, custom or based on spreadsheets. Additionally, the surveys suggested that users felt that the deployed solutions were more than effective, on average, in terms of meeting their business needs. However, they also suggested that the total cost of ownership (TCO) of their software solutions in the wholesale trading and risk management business functions had proven to be somewhat higher than they had originally anticipated. Similarly, among those that measured Return on Investment (ROI) for software solutions in this area, most felt that their ROI from their ETRM software solutions was "average" or "better than average".

Figure 3.1 Effectiveness of and satisfaction with ETRM software solutions

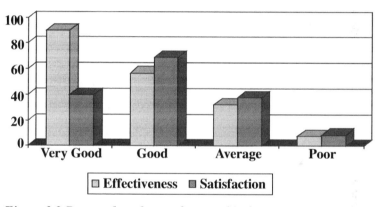

Figure 3.2 Reported total cost of ownership for ETRM software solutions

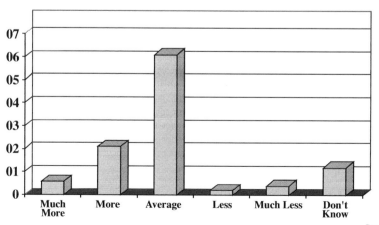

Although the reported satisfaction and the effectiveness levels reported for ETRM software solutions in general were quite good, there was also evidence that total cost of ownership (TCO) was often higher than originally anticipated. In fact, when taken in conjunction with other findings in these two studies, the data suggests that reported satisfaction levels with solutions might reflect lowered expectations on the part of the users. When replacement rates, reasons for replacement and, lack of overall solution integration is also taken into account, the picture painted by the study's results overall are a good deal more negative.

Figure 3.3 Reported ROI for ETRM software solutions

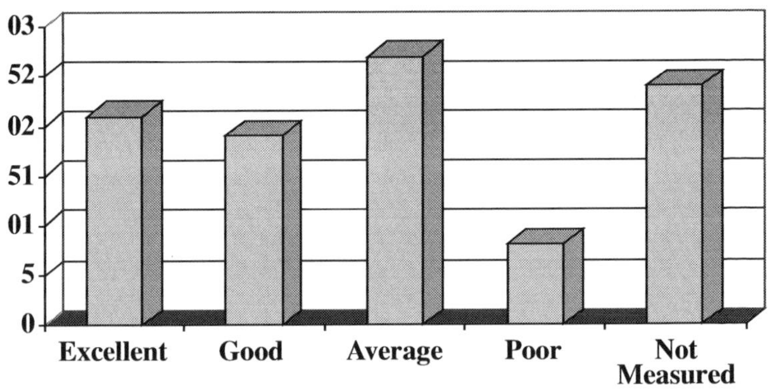

On average, vendor-provided solutions appeared to fare better than internally-developed applications in terms of both TCO and ROI but inferior to internally-developed solutions in terms of their effectiveness at meeting business requirements. Internally developed solutions, on the other hand, often required a larger amount of support thus reducing TCO but increasing the sense of effectiveness for these solutions.

High Historical Software Replacement Rates

The volatility of the energy trading business is reflected in the plans to both replace their ETRM software solutions and in their reasons for doing so discovered by the studies. The studies found that users would like to replace 30% of electric power and 48% of natural gas installed ETRM software applications. For electric power ETRM users, some 23% expected to replace within 2-years as compared to 18% for natural gas ETRM users. Conversely, 55% of electric power ETRM users had no plans to replace while just 21% of natural gas ETRM users had no plans to replace.

The difference in replacement plans between electric power and natural gas ETRM users seems to be explained by several other findings in the studies as follows;

- Many natural gas marketing, scheduling and risk systems are older both in terms of overall architecture and functionality. In fact, many respondents were using unsupported vendor solutions that had been heavily customized and had reached end of life. This is not surprising, since as we discovered in earlier chapters of this book, it was the natural gas wholesale markets that were de-regulated first.
- The natural gas study also indicated that IT budgets were projected to be flat or negative for the subsequent three years. This leaves users with older systems that they would like to replace but with no identified budget to do so.
- On the electric power side of the business new regulatory and structural changes seemed to be driving plans for software replacement.

These replacement rates seem remarkably high when compared to replacement rates in other software categories across the energy industry. For example, UtiliPoint found a Customer Information Systems (CIS) replacement rate of around 16 percent in 2004 and that reflected increased demand for CIS software over previous years (2003: 10 percent; 2002: 5 percent).

Some insight into these high replacement rates can be obtained from a review of the reasons for replacement provided by respondents. Most of those planning to replace their software reported that their current solution could not meet new business requirements and, in some instances, could not meet existing business requirements. A secondary motivation was the lack of or threatened lack of continuing support for their software solutions.

These results confirm that the rapid pace of change in business requirements in the industry results in difficulty keeping pace with those changes in ETRM software solutions – however provided. Even when providers are able to keep up with industry changes, it results in a need for frequent upgrades and users may become increasingly overwhelmed by the pace of those upgrades and fall behind. Once behind, users find it difficult to catch up and may eventually be forced to replace the application as a cheaper and more effective way of keeping up with business requirements.

Figure 3.4: ETRM Replacement Plans

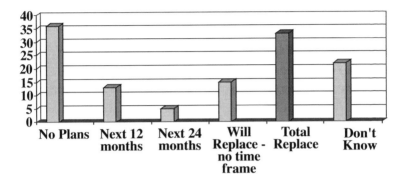

The decision to replace is not taken lightly by users as a result of the costs incurred in selecting and implementing a new software solution. Often, the potential for ETRM replacement is also reduced due to prior negative experiences with software implementation reflecting a "once bitten, twice shy" attitude. In fact, other UtiliPoint research has shown that it is actually more difficult than might initially be thought to replace an incumbent vendor largely because of this reason.

Gartner Group has captured this effect well in its "Hype Cycle" (Figure 3.5). UtiliPoint has little doubt that the ETRM software category is only now beginning to recover up the "slope of enlightenment" from the "trough of disillusionment" as the software class as a whole begins to mature. Further evidence for this rationale is presented below.

The sample represented in the surveys also demonstrates that this is now becoming largely a replacement market for software (i.e. new software sales or developments will be replacing legacy solutions). Vendor-provided software now accounts for between 40 and 60% of the market depending on the specific application area. The most mature application areas are generally deal capture, position keeping, scheduling, risk management and settlement and invoicing and these application areas are most often provided by a vendor solution. However, smaller energy companies are often using spreadsheets to provide an ETRM solution.

Figure 3.5 The Hype Cycle after Gartner Group

1.0 The Hype Cycle

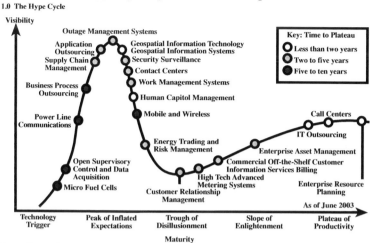

Source: Gartner Research (June 2003)

The replacement rates indicated by the studies broadly agree with other independent research undertaken by UtiliPoint in the past and readily demonstrate the volatility in the industry both from a business requirements point of view as well as from a vendor stability perspective. Additionally, it suggests an on-going level of dissatisfaction with ETRM software solutions generally that is perhaps understandable in the light of the history of the industry supporting the concept that the Gartner hype cycle has relevance in this industry.

An analysis of the relative proportions of virgin and replacement markets is also useful in gaining an insight into the solution landscape. A virgin market is defined as a market that utilizes internally-built, spreadsheet-based or manual processes and would be expected at some point to license mature commercial systems. A replacement market is one in which users already use commercial applications but may be open to replacing them with new commercial applications for a particular set of reasons.

The studies show that about 60 percent of the traditional trading, transaction and risk management software space is now a replacement market in a wholesale power marketing context. By comparison, something less than 40 percent of the asset-oriented aspects of wholesale power marketing are now replacement markets. Additionally, relatively new business processes requiring systems support such as hedge accounting and credit management, as might be expected, display a greater proportion of home-grown solutions due to the reduced maturity of commercial software in those application areas.

Figure 3.6 Virgin Versus Replacement Markets by Application Area

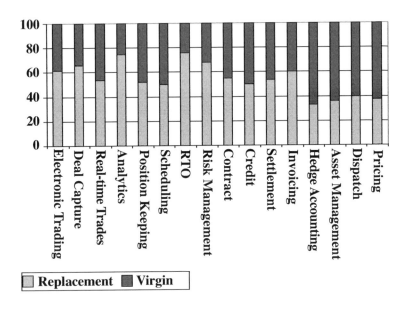

Software Solutions and Spreadsheet Usage

Part of the success of installing an ETRM software solution in today's energy trading world is based on whether it can eliminate or reduce the organization's reliance on spreadsheets. With the pressures facing energy companies around improved corporate governance, including the requirements of Sarbanes-Oxley, spreadsheets cannot be relied upon for accuracy, transparency or auditability. The vast majority of software solutions in use – whether licensed from a vendor or internally built – fail to eliminate spreadsheet use according to the results of the two studies. There is no obvious correlation between any particular software product/vendor and its ability to help with spreadsheet elimination. In all instances where a respondent indicated that a particular software product had eliminated spreadsheet use, there was at least one other respondent using the same solution that said it had not. This suggests that the ability of a particular software solution to eliminate spreadsheets is based either on its degree of fit to requirements initially and/or the overall success of the implementation approach. Today, spreadsheets continue to be used extensively across the marketing and risk management business functions with around half of the respondents saying that spreadsheet usage was "widespread" across the enterprise.

The continued and widespread use of spreadsheets in marketing and risk management is also evidenced by the distribution of software solutions to support the various business functions. Spreadsheet solutions, either stand-alone, or as a supplement to other software applications, are indicated to occur most commonly in the following application areas;

• Position keeping
• Power scheduling/pre-scheduling
• Credit management
• Settlement
• Gas storage

However, spreadsheets are used ubiquitously to support business activities across all the application areas reviewed in these studies even if just for ad hoc reporting. One participant even suggested that spreadsheet use was so ubiquitous that users often resorted to using and maintaining "secret" spreadsheet applications.

The importance of an overall IT infrastructure or architecture that provides integration and flexibility to the wholesale trading function is demonstrated by the total number and heterogeneity of the different software applications used to support the wholesale energy marketing business functions. Every respondent, no matter of what size and complexity, runs multiple different systems and modules including Excel spreadsheets, internally developed systems and software licensed from vendors. The number of systems in use by respondents ranged from three to 13 separate applications for electric power and one to ten for natural gas. Discounting the use of internally developed systems and/or Excel-based solutions, less than one third of the respondents utilized a single vendor to supply the key components of its solution (deal capture through scheduling to invoicing) while the remainder utilized a multi-vendor strategy. Even when a primary vendor-based solution was used, other applications were also often required for specific business functions.

Typically, energy firms have been faced with either pursuing a best of breed strategy or a single vendor option. In the first case, the energy company buys or builds software components for each business function and then attempts to integrate those best of breed modules together. In the latter case, the integration infrastructure is provided by the single vendor. Plainly, the concept of a sole provider and hence a vendor-provided (or bundled) integration framework is a fallacy and all respondents in these studies are utilizing a best of breed strategy at some level. By using this approach, the IT department must also devise and implement an integration strategy through both business processes and/or an IT architecture.

Surprisingly, the studies indicated that more than half of all respondents lacked any type of coherent IT architecture to provide this much needed integration and connectivity, with most relying instead on the provision of manual interfaces between systems.

Figure 3.7 Integration levels in Electric Power between ETRM Application Areas

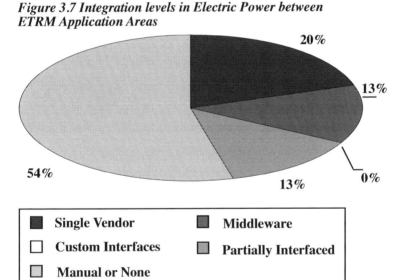

The level of complexity of the application architectures combined with the lack of IT infrastructures designed to support integration and connectivity between applications, is both surprising and concerning. The demands placed on IT departments in maintaining a poorly integrated and heterogeneous environment while being positioned to adequately respond to the ongoing needs of the business, are high. Similarly, the company's ability to comply with the requirements of Sarbanes-Oxley, good financial reporting and other corporate governance requirements will be potentially compromised through the lack of integration.

Summary

The current state of the ETRM software installed base in North America as indicated by UtiliPoint research comprises heterogeneous application portfolios that are either un-integrated or poorly integrated. There are numerous users using older vendor-provided solutions that are now reaching end of life and are set for replacement while there are entire subsets of the market that are still virgin territory and rely on spreadsheet-based solutions. To some extent, looking at the installed base is like reviewing the history of the energy trading industry and the software vendors and products.

The problem with this is that new regulations and structural change in the energy industry cannot be readily supported by the installed base however it was provided. Energy companies and their shareholders are exposed to control weaknesses, reporting deficiencies and more. This is an untenable situation and one that is driving a new level of demand for ETRM software through 2005 and 2006. The good news however, is that ETRM vendors have made considerable strides in terms of the overall strength and maturity of the ETRM software that they offer from overall architecture to functional coverage.

FOUR

BUSINESS DRIVERS IN ENERGY TRADING AND RISK MANAGEMENTI

Introduction
By Dr. Gary M. Vasey,
UtiliPoint International

The wholesale energy trading industry has evolved and grown rapidly over the past several years in response to various forms of deregulation and innovation among industry players. It is now clear, that as a result of the problems that the industry faced in 2001, it is still evolving. Today's energy company is faced with numerous new challenges originating from the recent collapse of the mega-merchants. These changes can be defined as occurring in two key areas – industry restructuring and new regulations - both sets of industry changes have had and continue to have a significant impact on ETRM software requirements and architectures.

In the first instance, it was the vacuum created by the demise of the merchants that has resulted in a structural change in energy markets. As the industry struggled with the collapse of the Merchants, many traditional energy companies, those with assets, abandoned plans to create non-regulated speculative trading arms and instead, returned to an asset heavy model where 'trading' was limited to trading around its assets (Figure 4.1). For a while, energy commodity trading markets displayed reduced liquidity and less volume as the energy industry distanced itself from speculative trading and, in some instances, the more exotic derivative instruments. However, someone had to fill the void created by the exit of the Merchants and over the last 18-months, the investment banks, hedge funds and, to some extent, multi-national oil companies have progressively entered energy trading. As energy prices and volatilities have gone up those initial 'speculators' have seen profits rise exponentially. Recently, for example, BP announced trading profits of close to $2 billion for 2004. This has simply attracted more speculators into energy markets so that today, more than 130 energy commodity hedge funds are active as compared to 10 just two-years ago.

As a result of this there is now a dichotomy of emerging requirements for ETRM software. While all players require functionality to capture data up to and including the actual trade, only the physical players require the functionality to capture and manage the physical transactions. Additionally, while regulations such as Sarbanes-Oxley, FAS 133 and recommendations such as those originating from the CCRO have had the effect of standardizing business processes in areas such as deal capture, position keeping and risk management, the transaction management side has remained both commodity and location specific. Of course, there are no single set of standards for any of these businesses processes but there are now sufficient guidelines and regulations to impact certain requirements in such a way as to create pseudo-standards.

Meanwhile, for physical players, the situation has become even more complex. Each energy commodity is potentially delivered via different transportation methods and each transportation method requires a unique solution whether that is by pipeline with the nominations and confirmations process to consider or, by tanker, with the requirement for a wide variety of associated documentation. Further, some energy commodity markets are still going through structural design and those requirements remain uncertain. For electric power providers in North America, for example, each regional market is developing its own structure and participation rules for physical and financial trading requiring specific market communication tools.

Figure 4.1: Energy Industry Structural Change Following the Collapse of the Merchants

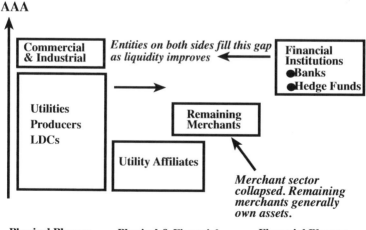

Secondly, new regulations and rules such as Sarbanes-Oxley, FAS 133, increased attention on risk management from Standard & Poors, as well as the self-regulation requirements emerging from the Committee of Chief Risk Officers (CCRO) are having a significant impact on ETRM software. These new rules and regulations introduce both new areas of requirement such as hedge accounting, for example, but also add additional requirements to existing applications ranging from the need for additional security to better support of business processes and audit trails. Today's vendor-provided software offerings are closer than ever before at being able to meet many, if not all, of these requirements however many users are still stuck with older versions of software that do not offer these features.

This section will look in more detail at some of these business trends as drivers of new functionality in ETRM software systems, in the deployment of new architectures and software delivery and, the broader context of ETRM solutions.

Structural Change in Energy Markets and its Impact on ETRM Requirements

Industry structural change following the collapse of the energy merchants has had a significant impact on ETRM vendors and solutions. As utilities, producers, and other holders of physical assets moved to a more asset-centric business model, a new breed of speculative energy traders have emerged in the form of investment banks, hedge funds and the multinational oils. As a result, there are now really two sets of requirements for ETRM software; one for those who essentially need to manage up to the actual trade (speculative traders) and one for those that have to actually manage the physical side of the business or move the molecule (asset-centric players).

The 'Speculators'

While natural speculators may take a risk position based on their understanding and view of the market the asset heavy side of the business is more concerned with dealing with their naturally long or short position with minimal risk and with maximizing their asset's profitability. The more speculative side of the industry needs to be able to manage market data, capture and process trades and engage in sophisticated risk management and market modeling. The asset heavy side of the industry needs to perform some of those functions but it also has to track and reconcile the movement of the molecules too.

Many investment banks active in energy markets, though not all, are essentially speculating in energy derivatives as opposed to trading the underlying physical commodity. Bank of America, for instance, is limiting itself to the buying and selling financial contracts and avoiding the actual delivery of power. As such, the financial institution is allocating seven of its 55 traders in New York to its power trading team.

The combination of price volatility and trading talent created as a result of the collapse of the mega-merchants is also providing an opportunity for hedge funds. D.E. Shaw and Citadel have hired staff from the former energy trading operations of Aquila and another fund, Alpha Energy Partners L.P., is being run by former energy traders from American Electric Power. In fact, more than 130 hedge funds seem set to play in energy commodities markets and will bring more risk capital to bear in those markets. The impact of their trading activity is already evident.

Hedge funds bring more than risk capital to the market. They also bring increased sophistication, liquidity, a risk culture and trading acumen. Seeking new opportunities to obtain greater returns, hedge funds see energy markets as potentially providing that opportunity. Likewise, investment banks have a risk trading culture, deep pockets and access to both physical and financial traders. Even energy companies with surviving trading arms are now often partnering with investment banks to sustain and improve trading operations while obtaining access to increased expertise, stronger balance sheets, more sophisticated tools and risk capital. TXU's deal with Credit Suisse First Boston to create a joint venture for energy trading and marketing services and Merrill Lynch's agreement to buy Entergy-Koch's energy trading business serve as examples.

Impact on Energy Markets and Software Requirements

The return of speculative trading in energy commodities brings with it significantly increased liquidity, more sophisticated financial instruments, and risk management approaches/strategies. To support trading activities, firms will need to invest in improved expertise, resources and tools around all aspects of risk management, including credit risk management. The potential for increased sophistication in energy derivatives trading will ultimately require more robust and scalable trading systems combined with increasingly sophisticated financial risk management tools. The good news for software vendors is two-fold. Firstly that a new software market is opening rapidly with an appetite for risk management tools for investment banks and hedge funds; and secondly, there will be a ripple effect across the entire industry that will drive demand in existing markets.

Indeed, announcements by SunGard Kiodex suggests that it has been one early beneficiary of this need for risk management tools to support the energy trading activities of both investment banks and hedge funds. The company has signed a number of new hedge fund subscribers. Kiodex President, Raj Mahajan, offers four primary reasons for his company's success in attracting investment banks and hedge funds. These include an implementation "measured in days"; lower total cost of ownership as a result of its subscription-based model; Kiodex's forward curves that provide accurate and reliable marks for more than 120 locations globally in crude oil, refined products, natural gas, electric power and metals; and the multi-factor model risk engine at the heart of his company's software.

Increased liquidity in the markets is one aspect of this activity that may have the effect of invigorating volume and transaction growth while the banks' and funds' good credit should improve confidence in counterparty credit risks. The net result may well be increased trading activities industry-wide, and certainly, this may stimulate increased demand for transaction and risk management systems industry wide benefiting the broader vendor community.

Asset Heavy Players

Tracking the energy trading space over 2005, UtiliPoint research has shown that the dichotomy in requirements between "speculators" and other asset heavy energy companies is growing. While there is considerable overlap between the "speculators" and the utilities in the sense that some "speculators" own assets and some utilities and producers "speculate," there are still two distinct sets of requirements, even in a single organization.

The dichotomy has reflected itself in the wide number of available solutions for trade capture, position keeping and risk management and a number of more specialist and niche-oriented vendors that are focused on logistics, scheduling, asset optimization, generation dispatch and so on. While a small number of vendors can provide most of this functionality it is not always best in class and so many users end up with a number of different applications in place to support their business requirements. Indeed, a recent study of applications used to support electric power wholesale trading in North America found that on average, each marketer or utility was utilizing between 6 and 12 different applications[2] . This same stud found that more than half of the surveyed companies were also

[2] IT Benchmarking at North American Power Marketers, UtiliPoint International Report, 2004

using manual interfaces between these applications to manage the business. In today's era, this is a significant business risk.

E&P Companies Re-enter the Markets

Exploration and production companies have historically been in business to explore for, find and produce energy commodities. They face many business challenges as they seek to economically replace reserves, produce sustained cash flows and earn a profit for stakeholders. The sudden absence of large merchants significantly increased their challenge. To provide for reserves, cash flows and profit, E&P companies are now including in their marketing strategies a re-entry into the wholesale markets. In today's volatile oil and natural gas markets, this means rebuilding marketing groups and developing effective risk management strategies to protect against price, credit, supply and other significant risks and exposures.

Producers must once again focus on the operational and tactical management of the company's portfolio of assets and make business decisions that take the best advantage of any profit opportunity window that the market provides while protecting against the downside. To meet profit targets, producers often need to take controllable risks. Naturally, producers are also required to hedge against price volatility and operations risks to preserve capital for reserve replacement and to reduce earnings volatility. When combined with new requirements to comply with Sarbanes-Oxley, FAS 133 accounting standards, and to take on-board best practice such as those suggested by the CCRO, the producer is certainly faced with a new and daunting challenge.

To meet this challenge, producers need software solutions that adequately support their business processes and provide the accurate and timely information needed to optimally manage the business while providing stakeholders with increased confidence in management reports. Historically, software solutions were available to support producers in their marketing endeavors but, as the merchant segment matured, and many producers chose to outsource marketing and risk management functions to the merchant, vendors responded accordingly. Not surprisingly, few physical transaction management solutions for producer marketers has been brought to market for some years.

For many producers, the absence of a modern marketing and risk management software platform has prompted a growing reliance on spreadsheets. However, the use of spreadsheets to manage such a critical aspect of a producer's business is also fraught with issues and risks. Spreadsheets offer little protection against trading or credit limit breaches, require multiple entries of the same data, which wastes time and effort, and provide no audit trail that can be used to document a particular set of actions. Furthermore, spreadsheets are subject to human error with no way to validate entered transaction data.

Producers are now required to perform their own scheduling and capacity management of their natural gas production for delivery to their new customers. Scheduling has always been a complex task requiring multiple transportation agreements with pipelines, submitting and confirming nominations, continuous imbalance management and monthly reconciliations. With the additional responsibilities associated with storage capacity management and the need to comply with each individual pipeline's data and processing requirements, the scheduling function would best be served by software tools that are easy to use and intuitive.

Another emerging requirement specifically for producers is the ability to not just manage transactions associated with sales activities, but to also tie volumes, sales revenues and costs back to the interest owners in the assets. Traditionally production and revenue allocation has been performed by other software systems within the enterprise requiring an interface or manual data entry with sales and cost information. For producers in particular, the demise of the merchant has created a new requirement for software to support their re-entry into marketing production. Another effect of the collapse of the merchant segment of the industry has been to create an array of complex new rules, regulations and business practices that requires software that meets these new requirements. Lack of investment in oil and natural gas transaction management software until recently means that there are few software solutions that can meet the needs of the today's producer.

LDC's Face New Challenges in Supply and Price Management

At the other end of the value chain, the LDC, or gas utility, is also subject to a variety of new business issues. Customer choice programs in some states have created additional responsibilities for LDCs. They may now have to handle nominations, forecasts, imbalances, settlements and supplier billings. Even for those unaffected by retail deregulation, reliability of supply remains a key requirement. With increasing scrutiny from federal, state and local regulatory agencies, LDCs have to assure reliability of supply at a prudent cost or face further scrutiny in attempting to justify rate increases. Indeed, the LDC is now under pressure to justify not just its rates but also costs, acquisition strategies, auditing and reporting of exposures and mitigation strategies deployed.

Many LDCs are comprised of multiple lines of business or subsidiaries, both regulated and non-regulated. Typically, each of these businesses utilizes different business systems and requires multiple data input standards as a consequence. If electric power generation is involved then these issues can be compounded by the need to manage multiple energy commodities that can be used as fuel (i.e. crude oil, coal, propane, etc.). Facing many of the same regulatory and business practice guidelines as the rest of the energy industry, LDCs are also subject to increased counterparty credit, price and supply risks. As a result, they must also consider asset structures, asset operating strategies, fuel purchase arrangements, financial hedges and other contract structures to both mitigate these risks and optimize their cost structures on a timely basis. However, because of the multitude of disparate systems in place across business units, LDC management may find it extremely difficult to access timely and accurate data

Public utility regulatory commissions have increased their scrutiny of LDC and gas utility justifications for gas cost and customer fees. In order that management can respond with timely and accurate information, LDCs and gas utilities, now more than ever before, require new software solutions to adequately support these important business processes at the enterprise level. They cannot continue to rely on spreadsheets and disparate systems to manage their business effectively.

There have been very few commercially available solutions for LDCs to support their gas procurement and risk management activities. Most of the early gas marketing and risk management software packages targeted other industry segments such as producer marketers and these never truly met the specific requirements of the LDC. And what remains of these early software packages is now rapidly reaching end-of-life is unsupported or offered by very small software vendors. As a result, LDCs have often managed using a combination of home-grown spreadsheets combined with in-house developed solutions, or, in some cases, a third-party solution.

Electric Utilities Must Manage Assets and Operate in Regional Markets

The back to basics approach of many electric utilities places the emphasis back on the optimized use of their generation and other assets. At the same time, the emergence of the independent systems operator (ISO) or regional transmission operator (RTO), has created a number of regional markets for power across North America each having its own data exchange and settlement characteristics. This has created increased complexity in terms of managing transactions and risk but also makes for complex business processes that need to be supported. Depending upon the location and nature of its generation assets, an electric utility can have numerous fuel needs. Each fuel has to be procured and exposure to price and other risks mitigated.

To operate its generation assets on an optimized basis, the electric utility has to plan for and understand demand and price changes in its markets on a minute-to-minute basis. To do so, it requires a suite of software tools to project load, demand, regional market conditions, prices and more. In addition to procuring fuel in wholesale energy markets, it may chose to sell excess capacity in wholesale markets too. It is exposed to risks on both sides of the generation facility and not just price risk. It also needs to trade in real-time as market conditions change and adjustments are required to be made. In scheduling electric power, the utility may be dealing with numerous regional markets each of which has different standards for data exchange, different rules to comply with and different settlement procedures.

As a consequence of its business dynamics, electric utilities may also find the traditional model of an ETRM software package somewhat lacking as discussed in more detail below. ETRM systems have to be supplemented with a range of other software tools and many may be spreadsheet-based ranging from market communications through to real-time trading. UtiliPoint research shows that the average power marketer in North America can use between 6 and 12 separate applications to support these business processes and from a controls point of view, these applications are often poorly integrated.

Speculators and Asset Heavy – an emerging dichotomy in Requirements

"Speculators" in energy trading usually take a view on where they believe the market is going either through fundamental analysis or using trend following models or a combination of both. Often they will engage in complex trading scenarios that require dissagregation of the risk elements involved making a particular trading strategy a number of trans-actions for the purposes of recording the deal and its risk attributes in a software system. They may see both their view on the market and their approach to risk management as competitive differentiators. For the "speculator," system architectures may be "custom" and contain several in-house components. While they may use vendor-provided applications they want to also be able to replace particular applications as required and plug them in to the overall solution. "Speculators" may also gather market intelligence and information to perform proprietary analytics and to develop trading strategies. Finally, they may use more financial instruments in conducting trading.

On the other hand, asset heavy utilities and producers are more usually concerned with managing a naturally long or short position with minimized risk, best use of capital employed and optimized use of their assets. They may engage in hedging to manage price risk but much of their business involves dealing in physical markets and will mean delivering or taking delivery of the physical commodity. Therefore, they also have to deal with the complexities of moving and managing the molecule including scheduling, documentation and accounting for losses or other discrepancies. Their requirements then include a host of transaction management needs that add complexity to the business and their required software solution. UtiliPoint research shows that asset heavy players often regard IT as an expense to the business as opposed to a competitive advantage in the case of the "speculators" and are often heavy users of vendor-provided software.

While the above is a simplification of the dichotomy it serves to highlight some of the different needs of asset heavy and asset light companies in energy trading, transaction and risk management (ETRM) software. In reality, the asset heavy companies have a much broader and more complex set of requirements by virtue of the fact that they primarily engage in trading the physical commodity.

Physical Complexity

The physical side of the energy trading business is still tremendously complex. In electric power, North American power markets have emerged in ISO/RTO form and each has its own rules and data requirements. These are essentially regional markets that to some extent are still developing although some markets such as PJM and others are more mature than others with respect to standards, procedures and data transfer needs. Gas markets in North America are no less complex since almost every pipe has its own proprietary extension to GISB for confirmation and nomination handling and other interactions between shipper and pipe. Crude oil trading requires significant documentation around the shipping function and even coal comes in various qualities and specifications that need to be tracked and managed. In short, the physical side of the business simply requires much more tracking, accounting and management that translates into complex applications to handle scheduling, movement, quality and so on. It is these significant complexities that often present the biggest challenge for users in terms of software solutions.

Evolution of ETRM Software

ETRM software has evolved in North America over the last 10-15 years in step with industry changes however, it has also developed somewhat along the lines of financial trading and risk management systems with an emphasis on straight through processing. Since the deregulation of North American power markets, the growing awareness of the need to manage risks has brought in a number of financial trading and risk management vendors who have developed energy-oriented software and, during the merchant era in particular, were quite successful in marketing those software solutions into the energy industry. In fact, the merchant era actually could be argued to have driven the ETRM software requirement towards a more financial trading and risk management model.

Of course, there are more than 65 vendors offering various flavors of ETRM software today and not all of them have taken this more financial and risk-centric approach. There are significant numbers of ETRM vendors that have focused on attempting to solve specific issues related to the physical complexities of the business and some offer best in class niche requirement software. The larger and better known vendors have all to some extent moved to solve some of the issues in the business developing scheduling and other functionality in response to customer requirements. What is now required is a broader class of software, particularly for electric utilities, that caters for the expanded needs of asset-heavy entities.

What is Asset ETRM?

The key difference between the "speculators" and asset-heavy companies engaged in energy trading is the requirement for the transaction management component in ETRM. The emphasis for "speculators" is really in capturing the trade and managing the risk while for asset-heavy companies it is in moving and managing the physical commodity (See Table 4.1).

UtiliPoint analysis suggests that there are two significant new areas of functionality required by asset-heavy users of ETRM systems. The first occurs prior to trading and involves market analysis and forecasting including load forecasting and price forecasting in particular regional commodity markets along with asset optimization modeling. The need is to optimize the use of assets against usage and outage trends in regional markets. It helps determine the most profitable way in which to manage assets given the market needs. It also has a real-time trading component to it in the sense that adjustments need to be made in real-time through the day as market dynamics change. The second area is in market communication particularly in regional power markets where bidding, dispatch, scheduling, ISO communication, settlements and reconciliations are needed. Figure 4.1 is a simplified comparison of "traditional" ETRM with our view of the emerging need for an Asset ETRM solution.

Today, many of the larger software vendors in the ETRM space offer solutions which are a hybrid of these two admittedly extreme variants of an ETRM solution. Other software vendors who specialize in market communication, load forecasting and other asset oriented requirements are integrated or interfaced with the primary ETRM system to provide the overall solution.

Table 4.1 - Requirement summary for ETRM users

Up to the Trade	*Moving & accounting for the commodity*
• Deal Capture	• Pre-scheduling/Schedule/Logistics
• Position Keeping	• Physical Settlement & Invoicing
• Trade Analytics	• Volume Management
• Market Data/Analysis	• Reporting
• Risk Analytics	• Marketing Communication
• Risk Reporting	• Noms/Confirmations
• Counterparty Credit	• Asset Management
• Trade Settlement & Invoicing	• Dispatch
• Data Mining	• User Decision Support for Optimal
• Trade and Risk Controls	Operations
"Speculators"	**Asset Heavy Users**

UtiliPoint analysis and research shows that a new requirement for ETRM is emerging to cater for the asset heavy side of the industry. Today, these requirements are either provided by the ETRM vendor or through niche best in class software components from other vendors. We expect that over time some ETRM vendors will migrate their solutions to more fully cater for asset heavy utilities and producers through the creation of integrated suites of modules that better serve that side of the industry while others will continue to primarily serve the more speculative side of the business.

New Natural Gas Solutions

A number of new natural gas systems have recently come to market from a variety of software vendors. Many of the existing natural gas marketing systems were introduced in the mid-nineties and are on older technology platforms. Additionally, many of them do not fully reflect the structure of the natural gas business that has emerged since the collapse of the merchant segment of the industry. For producers, there have also been few introductions of new production and revenue accounting systems in the last 10 years.

While there are a number of software vendors offering highly usable natural gas systems, vendors including Quorum Business Solutions, SolArc, Triple Point Technologies, and SunGard Energy have announced or introduced new systems in recent months targeting different segments of the gas industry. Quorum has delivered a new pipeline management system, production volume management and, production and revenue accounting systems in recent months and is working on a new natural gas marketing system emphasizing more physical players. SunGard's new Entegrate platform includes comprehensive natural gas functionality and Triple Point Technologies has brought its GasXL software to market. SolArc is also working on a new gas marketing software solution. With existing natural gas solutions targeting various niche segments of the market from Allegro Development, OpenLink, Energy Softworx, TrinityApex, eSystems, DMS and SoftSmiths, the industry is experiencing something of a renaissance for natural gas software.

Figure 4.2 - Comparison Summary of ETRM and Asset ETRM Requirements

Traditional ETRM - More financial trading oriented

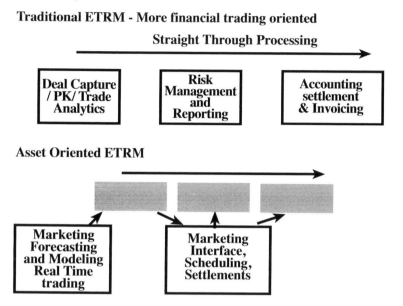

These new solutions deliver two fundamental requirements for the industry. First, they utilize newer architectures that deliver improved connectivity and easier integration capabilities to users and second, they often target segments of the industry that have specific requirements that have been underserved in the past such as gas producers or LDC's.

While more than 65 vendors[3] compete to provide some form of ETRM software, a small number of vendors dominate the market. Many of them have attained this position through the acquisition of other software companies and their products and, in fact, there is no single dominant product in the market. And even those products that do have a sizeable installed base, often owned by vendors that acquired them, may be rapidly reaching end of life.

---

[3]UtiliPoint's Directory of ETRM Vendors and Solutions, 2006, www.utilipoint.com

Table 4.2: High-level ETRM Requirements by Market Segment

High-Level Requirements	*Impacted Industry Segments*
Front Office: Deal capture, position keeping, market data, trader tools.	Utilities, Producers, Investment Banks Multi-National Oils, Commercial & Industrials, Hedge and other funds, Merchants/Marketers.
Middle Office: Risk Management, Risk Reporting, Risk Analysis, Stress Testing, Modeling, Credit Risk	Utilities, Producers, Investment Banks Multi-National Oils, Commercial & Industrials, Hedge and other funds, Merchants/Marketers.
Back Office: Settlement, Accounting, Invoicing, Credit management, AR, AP, GL.	Utilities, Producers, Investment Banks Multi-National Oils, Commercial & Industrials, Hedge and other funds, Merchants/Marketers.
Physical Transaction Management: Pre-scheduling, Scheduling, Asset Optimization, Dispatch, load forecasting and management.	Utilities, Producers, Investment Banks owning assets, Merchants/Marketers owning assets.
Physical Risk Management: Volume & delivery risk management & reporting	Utilities, Producers, Investment Banks owning assets, Merchants/Marketers owning assets

Summary

Industry structural changes since the merchant collapse have necessarily impacted ETRM software and the nature of solutions required and available to energy companies. At the highest level, the return to a more asset-centric business model by producers and utilities of various types and the entry of new speculators has essentially emphasized the different needs of these two groups. The key difference is that asset-heavy energy companies have to track, account for and manage the movement of the physical commodity and therefore have a level of complexity in their requirements for software over and above that of pure speculators.

Pure speculators with an emphasis on financial energy and risk position are able to take advantage of the availability of more financially-oriented ETRM software, often delivered as a hosted service by a vendor where trading volumes allow. For the asset-heavy side of the industry, the true requirements of an ETRM system depend on the nature and location of the assets employed in the business. Producers require functionality to provide particular reports, for example, as well as integration with field data and production & revenue reporting systems while electric utilities require regional market communications and analysis. The ETRM software market can then be seen as a set of 'niche' markets (Table 4.2). Each 'niche' market has a common set of requirements for an ETRM system but also has some specific requirements to deal with as well. This is what makes the ETRM software market so complex.

In reality, the ETRM software market is not so much a 'package' market but rather a custom software market where each energy company has a unique set of requirements at some level. However, many requirements are shared across the industry meaning that ETRM software solutions are package-based but also have to be highly configurable and adaptable to have a broader basis for their use. In many instances, the ETRM software also has to be supplemented with some peripheral customized additions.

ADAPTING TO RAPID CHANGE: ETRM SOFTWARE VENDORS FACE A CRUCIAL TEST: HELPING ENERGY COMPANIES THRIVE IN COMPLEX, VOLATILE MARKETS

By Eldon Klaassen,
CEO and Founder,
Allegro

Complexity and volatility have long been energy industry facts of life, and in recent years have been escalating. These factors place demands on companies to constantly adapt — and on vendors of energy trading, transaction and risk management (ETRM) software to deliver solutions that adapt as well. Thus the ability to keep pace with rapid change is one of the greatest challenges and opportunities in energy business software, today and for the foreseeable future.

Volatility can take many forms: price instability, new business strategies, the need to enter new markets or deal with traditional markets suddenly shifting. Change can mean facing aggressive new players, such as traders dealing in new financial instruments or countries securing resources to fuel fast growing economies. There are also mergers and acquisitions. Business deregulation, and tightening environmental regulation. New tax rules and tariff agreements. Shifting business alliances, new accounting practices, emerging coal and LNG technologies, and more.

Therefore as energy industry volatilities increase, so does demand for ETRM solutions that can keep pace with change. Software vendors who best understand what energy companies need, will deliver the most effective solutions. These vendors must address demand by delivering more flexible ETRM solutions for critical business activities such as managing risk, improving profitability, and ensuring regulatory compliance.

What does this challenge mean for the future of energy business software? What does the roadmap to fully adaptable ETRM look like?

To fulfill this roadmap, next-generation ETRM software must:

• enable new, more complex types of transactions yet to be created,

• support more complex logistical decisions,

• give users better understandings of volatilities and market dynamics,

- allow more flexible management of business processes,

- free users from the need for "information silos" by ensuring that all relevant processes and information can be readily integrated into the system,

- permit more efficient handling of variables such as constraints, tariffs, and fees,

- help companies accommodate change at any scale, from enterprise-wide reorganization to individual user preferences, and

- enable companies to deploy and modify ETRM solutions more quickly to keep pace with changing business imperatives.

A tall order. Yet these functional signposts on the roadmap are achievable in the near term with software technologies already at hand. They are "must have's" for next-generation ETRM software, and therefore warrant a closer examination.

Handling new types of transactions

Companies are gradually gaining deeper understandings of risks and opportunities embedded within new market dynamics. As these understandings grow, professionals are creating new types of physical and financial transactions. Each transaction type expresses a series of risks to be hedged and opportunities to be leveraged.

As volatile, complex markets create more risks and opportunities, the number of transaction types will rise. Thus markets are already seeing increases in transactions involving multiple commodities, swaps, swings and spreads, multi-leg options, multiple tiering price mechanisms, deals featuring FX and weather derivatives, and other complex features.

New, complex transaction types are commonly beyond the capabilities of today's software, thus requiring workarounds. For example, users may need to manually disaggregate a complex deal into a series of vanilla transactions. Taken together, such pseudo-transactions can represent a complex deal. For instance, a swap can be represented as two simultaneous buy-sell transactions. Even a simple physical deal with a ceiling or floor may need to be disaggregated into its component options.

Manually disaggregating deals into smaller pseudo-transactions invites complications, especially if a deal's terms are later modified. These smaller transactions can get out of sync, spawning discrepancies in contract management, accounting, settlement, invoicing, documentation, reporting, and regulatory compliance. While such discrepancies can be manually adjusted, this tactic often cascades into further discrepancies — defeating the purpose, and significantly reducing the advantage of using integrated ETRM software in the first place.

A similar situation arises when a company performs internal transactions, such as inter-book or inter-division deals. Next-generation ETRM software must adapt to properly represent any such deals, to ensure that financial statements are not skewed or reporting rules violated.

Managing physical processes

To fulfill the roadmap, next-generation ETRM software must guide increasingly complex physical decision-making in virtually every energy commodity, and help users structure and administer correspondingly complex physical contracts.

As in financial trading, advanced software must assist in determining optimal actions and predicting financial outcomes. It must also help users understand and manage risks associated with each physical process step, and support strategies to mitigate those risks.

For example, gas storage transactions may have ratcheting requirements determining how much product can be injected or withdrawn, as a function of the volume an asset holder already has in storage. Adaptable ETRM software can monitor contract utilization, enabling an asset holder to avoid over-injecting. It could also help asset holders fully leverage contractual terms, to avoid under-injecting or under-withdrawing when market conditions dictate modifying a long position.

As pipeline capacity similarly becomes constrained, transport and transmission pricing structures will likely become more complex as well. Further, if a company cannot move its gas on a particular pipe, other decisions may be required. Is there an alternate route? Another market? Liquidate the position, or hold? Adaptable ETRM software integrates interactive geographic maps, contract information and pipeline and market data to support and even propose optimal decisions.

Liquefied natural gas introduces additional complexities and volatilities. LNG transforms gas delivery from a continuous physical process to a batch process. LNG market dynamics — and the contracts that must reflect these dynamics and their specific risks — will increasingly resemble those of crude transported by ocean tanker. LNG physical contract provisions will focus on timing and delays associated with marine shipping. Related contracts must address unique requirements of LNG storage and regasification, and in some cases additional gas processing and fractionation.

The software must also adapt to associated taxes, fees, approval processes and documentation that are part of the transaction lifecycle and logistics management.

Predicting volatilities and optimal paths

Market volatilities impose the greatest stress on traders and risk managers who make physical and financial transaction decisions from day to day. Their need for improved decision support grows as markets become more complex and price instability persists.

Next-generation decision support must adapt by delivering superior analytics, simulation and optimization tools integrated with real time, streaming market data. Such tools give professionals better understandings of volatilities and market dynamics, and provide more accurate price curves and other forward views.

Users can quickly simulate the impact of different decisions and varying market conditions. Optimization routines can help select optimal paths of execution from the hundreds of permutations possible with multi-leg options. Risk managers can develop more effective hedging strategies for mitigating volatility effects.

Hedging and optimization require fully integrated information. For a production company this may include data communications with field, SCADA and treasury systems to clearly understand volumetric information and counterparty exposures. It may also include market data plus information from pipelines, ISOs, brokers and exchanges, enabling greater insight into risks such as volumetric, price and counterparty risk.

These and other information sources must be captured and applied with advanced analytical and decision support tools. To meet such a challenge, ETRM adaptability is crucial. Companies can then confront volatilities with the best available means to leverage opportunities within a chosen risk profile.

Accommodating process changes

As corporate policies, strategies, alliances and internal controls evolve, business processes evolve with them. Next-generation ETRM software must accommodate even the most complex changes.

These changes may be far-reaching, for example restructuring entire approval hierarchies, with approval paths and individual authorizations redefined throughout the enterprise. Such reorganizations also require new workflows for document drafts, redirecting confirmations and resetting automated alerts and reminders in integrated software.

The most flexible ETRM solutions will also allow companies to convey specified contractual obligations to a new party, for a specified time span or indefinitely from a specified date.

Embracing numerous variables

Companies continually face changes in taxation, fees, compliance rules, contractual stipulations and other variables. Adaptable ETRM software must allow users to define an unlimited number of variables such as brokerage, transport, and management fees, and demand charges.

The software must be able to employ standard or user-defined formulas to calculate the charges, logic gateways to determine when charges should apply, and allocation routines that express which party pays what portion of the charge, under what terms and in which currency.

In addition, deal-specific variables may include counterparty information, deal number, volume/quantity specifications (unit, frequency, rate), locations (multiple points of delivery), pricing formulas, product quality, duration, and supply and demand load shapes.

Adapting at any scale

The ETRM roadmap requires that adaptability be pervasive throughout the solution. The software must adapt to complexity and volatility at any scale — and at any point in the energy business — from facilitating mergers and acquisitions to enabling users to self-customize their digital workspace.

On an enterprise scale, solutions must accommodate mergers and reorganizations in which business relationships as well as processes are redefined. ETRM solutions must ease the task of integrating processes and information from disparate business units. It must adapt to new corporate policies, and regulatory and accounting changes.

Virtually every software vendor claims its product "works the way you do." Next-generation solutions will have to prove it. Flexibility must reach down to the individual, enabling the software to satisfy each user's productivity preferences, such as which information to display, how to arrange it on the screen, and which links will be most readily accessible.

Deploying and modifying solutions

In some cases, confronting change may require a company to deploy a new, more adaptable ETRM solution. A wise approach combines a component-based, service-oriented architecture with a phased implementation strategy. This combination permits early deployment of the most critically needed functionality, addressing the area where a company is experiencing the most pain.

Subsequent deployment phases follow a declining "pain gradient" until a total solution is achieved. Each phase adds functionality, returning value to the enterprise while seamlessly integrating into the full solution. Phased implementation using modular software components also allows the solution plan itself to be readily modified if market volatilities demand it.

Other capabilities

While this discussion focuses on the ability to adapt to change, advanced energy business solutions have many other important capabilities as well. Messaging, automated confirmations and alerts, shared calendars and related features facilitate collaboration among individual, teams and counterparties. Invoicing and settlement can be highly automated, enabling teams to efficiently manage backoffice complexity. Processes for accounting, reporting, audit, regulatory compliance, documentation (including version control) and archiving are similarly flexible, integrated and highly automated in advanced ETRM solutions.

Summary/conclusion

Multiple ongoing volatilities in markets, energy demand, types of deals, business relationships, company ownership, regulation and accounting practices will continue to drive the need for ETRM software that readily adapts to complexity and rapid change.

Adaptable ETRM software will enable companies to improve risk management and profitability by more effectively penetrating markets, creating and managing innovative contracts, trading in new instruments, and managing multiple commodities.

What type of software will have the far-reaching flexibility to adapt? The most likely candidates will share a basic underlying structure — a service-oriented architecture characterized by Web services and a large number of independent, easily integrated, modular software components. These characteristics provide a foundation that can satisfy the requirements of implementation, processes, transactions, logistics, efficiency, processes, adaptability at any scale, and implementation.

Further, adaptable ETRM solutions will accommodate rapidly changing business processes by separating the processes themselves from underlying data. A process, for instance, may consist of a contract review cycle including a draft, review, edit, re-review, approval and confirmation. Underlying data might specify who performs the review, makes edits, checks the edits, resubmits the document for approval, re-reviews the document, and releases it to subsequent processes.

Thus behind the scenes, adaptable software separately manages the processes and data, actions and the actors, and dynamically integrates them when users request it. While a user may see a reminder to review and approve a contract; the software sees the same message as a process map and applies separately stored attributes to it.

When applied throughout the solution, and combined with a service-oriented architecture and other technical features, this decoupling strategy can make next-generation software adaptable enough to keep pace with extreme complexity and volatility.

No one can predict with certainty what changes lay in store for the energy industry — this most volatile of major industries — in the next few months, let alone the next few years. However, one thing is certain: companies that more readily adapt to change will be the ones still standing, and prospering, at the end of the day.

FIVE

NEW REGULATORY CHANGES IMPACT ETRM REQUIREMENTS AND BUYING CRITERIA

While industry structural change has an impact on ETRM software so too do the regulations and attention paid to industry issues such as corporate governance, financial reporting accuracy and so on, that have emerged since the collapse of Enron. In fact, there are a number of regulations and initiatives that are today impacting the ETRM requirements of energy companies including the Sarbanes-Oxley Act, FAS 133 and equivalent standards for hedge accounting, the recommendations of the Committee of Chief Risk Officers (CCRO), counterparty credit issues and the movement by Standards & Poors to review risk management and controls across the industry, and more.

This section reviews many of these new issues and requirements by starting with a look at Enterprise Risk Management and the COSO framework, Sarbanes-Oxley and best practice, credit risk, FAS 133 and the S&P initiative. It concludes by looking at ETRM as an essential component in risk policy.

CONTEMPLATING ENTERPRISE RISK MANAGEMENT (ERM) COSO'S ERM FRAMEWORK – ENHANCING MANAGEMENT'S CAPABILITIES

By Cal Payne,
UtiliPoint International, Inc.

Risk is unavoidable.

Every business faces risks as it works towards the achievement of its strategic objectives. Those risks can be characterized as potential barriers to the successful execution of their respective strategies. The governance hierarchy of companies of all sizes, beginning with the Board and cascading down through the enterprise, has an obligation to recognize, quantify, and manage those risks. Who could argue against the validity of that concept? So how does an organization go about implementing an enterprise risk management program? While the task is challenging, the good news is that there are guidelines out there that organizations can rely on to affect an ERM program. The most widely recognized example to date is the work of the Committee of Sponsoring Organizations of the Treadway Commission (COSO) who has developed a "best practice" framework that companies can use as a template to implement an integrated company-wide risk management program.

First Things First

Who is COSO? COSO was established in 1985 to make recommendations to public companies, independent auditors, regulators (e.g. the SEC), and educational institutions regarding the factors that could lead to fraudulent financial reporting. They have since published definitive studies in other accounting/audit related topics. Among their offerings is their internal control framework that has been widely utilized for complying with the provisions of Sarbanes-Oxley. That work serves as a basic design that has been expanded by COSO to envelop the concepts central to enterprise risk management efforts.

Now that we know who COSO is, let's define enterprise risk management. ERM is a process that enables a company to identify, quantify, and manage the risks the organization faces across the enterprise within an established risk tolerance. The program must have the support of (and be initiated by) the board of directors, and be embraced by the senior management team, other key positions, and eventually personnel at all levels of the company. A properly designed and empowered program *enables the company to preserve and enhance shareholder value* while working towards the achievement of its strategic objectives. It sounds like pretty powerful stuff and if properly executed, certainly is.

Setting the Stage

To create the best opportunity for the implementation of a comprehensive ERM program, we need to think about the company's various risks on a portfolio basis across the entire organization. This is often a paradigm shift for many firms where individual risks are looked at in isolation rather than as a component of a basket or portfolio of risks. The portfolio approach allows the companies to aggregate risks to see if there are internal natural offsets as well as providing an opportunity to establish and look at the company's risk universe which can then be measured against the firm's overall risk tolerance/appetite.

The COSO Defined Process

COSO has attempted to summarize the ERM process with a pictorial representation referred to as the COSO Cube. Here they demonstrate the integrated nature of the approach linking the key categories of entity level objectives with eight components of their process (described below), showing its organization reach from the parent down through the subsidiary level.

Internal Environment – The ERM process must take into consideration the unique internal operations of the company itself. That environment incorporates the actions and philosophy of the Board of Directors, the company's established risk appetite or tolerance, its risk culture, values, organizational design/structure, delegated authorities, defined roles and responsibilities, as well at its management style. COSO describes a planning process that includes strategic, operations, reporting and compliance objectives. It is this internal environment that dictates how the ERM program will be designed and how effective its implementation will be.

Objective Setting – An ERM program should be designed to ensure the company has established a strategy and objectives that are consistent with its vision and mission statements and that the risks assumed in executing that strategy are within its recognized risk appetite. The ongoing objective setting process is accomplished in a manner that is consistent with those two parameters.

Event Identification – In order to effectively manage risk, you must first recognize that it exists. In order to affect this task, management of the firm must take into consideration various factors that originate both internally and externally to the company. The identification process should be a collaborative one, bringing representatives with different perspectives, experiences, and roles within the organization to focus on what risks the company faces.

Risk Assessment – Once we have identified risk(s), we have to assess their potential impact on the organization and the probability of their occurrence. This can be accomplished by the application of different quantitative and qualitative techniques.

Risk Response – Now that we have identified and assessed the risks to be managed, the next step is to determine if the aggregation of those risks are within the company's established risk tolerance. During this exercise, the company must review each risk and determine if they are willing to retain the risk identified, divest themselves of that risk, or seek a way to lay off all or a portion of it. If the decision is the later, a risk mitigation strategy needs to be derived that satisfies the company objective.

Control Activities – Control activities refers the policies, processes, and procedures that are put in place to help guarantee that the risk response strategies established are properly executed, that ongoing risks are managed within the established risk tolerances, and that the company stays in compliance with internal limitations.

Information and Communication – An integrated effort like ERM requires the aggregation of a substantial amount of data that is essential for the effective assessment and management of risk. In an optimal situation, that information would reside in a specialized system(s) and/or data bases where that information could be mined by those responsible for managing, analyzing, and monitoring the risks identified. This data aggregation capability creates the foundation that serves as the basis for communicating meaningful information across different levels of the organization including senior management and the board of directors.

Monitoring – The risk management program is monitored to measure progress and make whatever changes are necessary to increase its effectiveness. Approaches utilized include ongoing monitoring (e.g. daily) and periodic evaluations as part of a robust internal audit program as an example.

Another Perspective

This brief description really does not do the COSO framework justice, but it does serve as an introduction to a methodology that has generated some traction, resonating with boards, company leadership and outside constituencies (e.g. the rating agencies). From a personal perspective I like many of the components of COSO's approach however, by attempting to build on their previous work regarding the internal control framework, their approach sometimes feels like it is forced making the concept appear more complex and beaurocratic than necessary. My preference is for a slightly different representation that projects ERM as a continuous process. I have attempted to demonstrate that with a different graphic with functions that differ slightly from the COSO approach.

Figure 5.1: The Continuous ERM Process

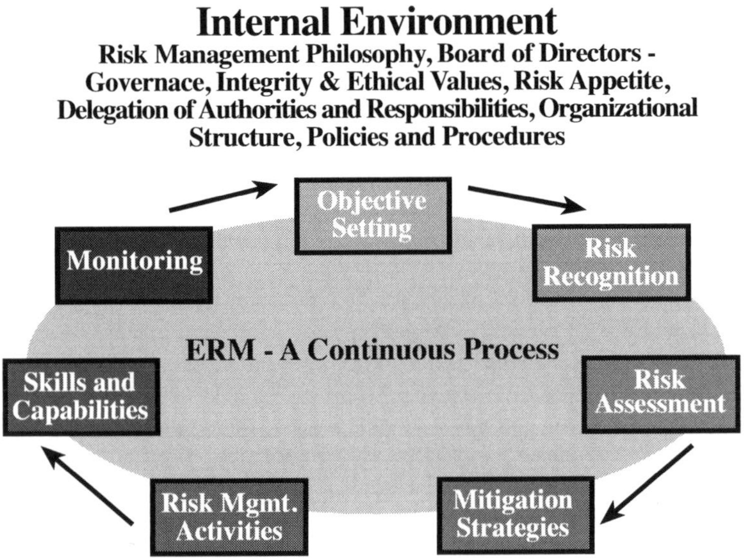
Internal Environment
Risk Management Philosophy, Board of Directors - Governace, Integrity & Ethical Values, Risk Appetite, Delegation of Authorities and Responsibilities, Organizational Structure, Policies and Procedures
Objective Setting
Risk Recognition
Risk Assessment
Mitigation Strategies
Risk Mgmt. Activities
Skills and Capabilities
Monitoring
ERM - A Continuous Process

In this model (like COSO's), the process must be designed to take into consideration the business' strategy and the reality of the company's internal environment. From that base, there are seven steps defined that represent the process. They are briefly described below.

Objective Setting – Set objectives takes into consideration high level goals that are aligned with the company's vision/mission, the effectiveness of the entity's operations (e.g. KPI's), internal/external reporting requirements, and compliance with applicable laws and regulations.

Risk Recognition – Identify the risk universe and events affecting the business that could act as a barrier to the achievement of its strategic goals and objectives.

Risk Assessment – Assess risks for their potential impact and the probability of their occurrence. This is a critical step in prioritizing the risks to be managed first.

Mitigation Strategies – Design risk mitigation strategies to reduce or eliminate risks the company chooses not to hold. Assign individuals or departments responsible for the execution of the strategies.

Risk Management Activities – Develop policies, processes, and procedures that help ensure risk mitigation strategies are effectively executed.

Skills and Capabilities – Determine the necessary capabilities and tools needed to accomplish the programs goals, e.g., personnel skill assessments, I.T. support requirements, and ensuring the appropriate delegated authority.

Monitoring – Plan for ongoing monitoring and scheduled reviews of ERM activities to measure the overall effectiveness of the effort. Provide documentation of the programs activities.

The process flows from step to step in a circular fashion and then begins again. The objectives and goal setting changes that occur from time to time in combination with our ability to effectively manage high priority risks, may shift our risk management efforts to focus on risks that were not previously targeted due to resource limitations. There will also be changes in our internal and external environment that may bring new risks to the forefront affecting the risk prioritization process. A robust ERM program is not ad hoc in nature, it is continuous, becoming part of the fabric of the organization.

While the implementation of an ERM program may seem daunting, it can be accomplished without the expense and investment in time associated with Sarbanes-Oxley compliance. What is required is the full support of management and the board. Helpful to the process is the appointment of owner/coordinator for the program like a Chief Risk Officer (there are other options) to direct the effort and the assignment of responsibility to individuals and departments to manage identified risks.

Many of the skills and capabilities to be effective in this endeavor already reside in most companies. Once the personnel are identified, their skills can be engaged to enable the process. You do not need to have an army of dedicated professionals to implement this concept. If well designed it will not be a bureaucratic burden added to people's existing workload. The process is scaleable and must be adjusted to the realities of the company involved. The one thing for sure is, that if properly executed, an ERM program can bring great value.

The Value Proposition

The benefits of a well designed ERM program are numerous and far reaching. ERM provides a systematic approach to identifying, assessing, and managing risk. By doing so, it enables a company to optimize its opportunities, growth, and the effective deployment of its capital. Other benefits include:

- The aggregation of risks and identification of opportunities across the enterprise to help improve results. The company is enabled to better manage key performance indicators, improve capital budgeting decisions, and optimize mergers and acquisitions.

- ERM will become an integral part of the decision making process for management enhancing supporting analysis and the quality of the outcome.

- Adoption of the program is consistent with emerging best practice standards regarding governance and the management of risk.

- It provides management with better information to make tactical and strategic decisions.

- The impact of negative events becomes more predictable, and due to the process in place, becomes more manageable.

- Opportunities can be better recognized, understood and then exploited.

- The overall cost of managing risk is optimized.

- Overall business performance is improved.

- Shareholder value is preserved and enhanced.

- Aligns a company's risk appetite with its strategy

- Corporate governance is enhanced through an improved oversight structure.

Figure 5.2 Example of an ERM Enhanced Governance Infrastructure

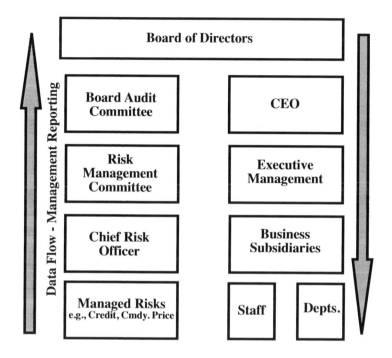

In the movement to enhance governance and increase corporate accountabilities, the new initiatives imposed and suggested have been questioned in terms of their perceived value to businesses and their shareholders. The emergence of ERM is an exception to those perceptions, where standards that are being suggested provide a valuable tool to board of directors and senior management teams as they work to preserve and enhance value for a company's various stakeholders. This is an initiative companies should embrace.

COMMERCIAL POLICY DEVELOPMENT: CORNERSTONE OF A "BEST PRACTICE" CONTROL INFRASTRUCTURE

By Cal Payne,
UtiliPoint International

Love or hate it, Sarbanes-Oxley has changed the way companies are doing business. Whether it's related to general areas of corporate governance, executive management/BOD liability or the rigor applied to the generation of the company's financial statements, the effects of Sarbanes-Oxley have been universal. Compliance with section 404 of the Act has forced the documentation and testing of policies, processes and procedures supporting the generation of a company's financial statements. OK, we have the accounting side of the business tied down, but what about the commercial side and its associated risks? That part of the business that generates the results we need to report.

There should be as much rigor applied here as there is in the proper accounting for the business. To do so is just plain good governance. The information, controls, and the messages that commercial policy document has daily impact over a much larger employee population than those involved in Sarbanes compliance. It is a formal document that should be widely circulated and understood throughout the organization.

What about a company's existing commercial policies? Is there alignment between the organization's stated strategy and business objectives and the policies that support that company's operations? Are they current? Do they reflect reality? Are they in compliance with emerging best practices standards? Do those supporting commercial polices even exist? These are important questions that need to be honestly answered.

If they do exist, they can be called many things which sometimes cause confusion when comparing one company's definition versus another. Some are all inclusive incorporating many aspects of a company's commercial operations and some take the form of multiple policies such as market risk, credit, trading and risk management. These types of policy pronouncements can be broadly defined as commercial and are outside of the classic procurement, human resources type polices that many companies utilize.

In general, commercial policies should be designed to support the underlying business strategies and institutionalize key best practice concepts within a comprehensive control environment/infrastructure. What design components are desired in a company's commercial policies? The document should speak to the business strategy, address governance, describe the organizational design and rationale for implementation, clarify individual department's/function's roles and responsibilities and detail the controls and limits surrounding the business to name some substantive topics. It should be readable and not in some legalese that the reader will have difficulty understanding. There must be some logic and organization to the presentation so employees can absorb the information, understand the overall concepts, and easily find the information they need to do their jobs.

Linking Policy and Strategy

So where do we begin? With all companies it begins with strategy. The clear articulation of strategy is critical to the achievement of the company's short and long term objectives. That strategy should be plainly stated in a comprehensive policy. What are we trying to accomplish as an organization? What are our objectives? Any commercial policies should be designed to support and facilitate the achievement of the company's objectives and established strategies. While this may seem obvious, my experience has shown there can be frequent disconnects between what a company's strategic objectives are and what the company's actual policies and practices reflect. This can be potentially dangerous. The last thing a board wants to deal with, or an investor wants to find out, is that what they thought was happening within an organization was inconsistent with reality. An example of a disconnect between policy and practice is the case where a company whose stated strategy is to optimize a portfolio of physical assets. The main objective of their commercial organization is to hedge their exposures with speculative position taking being strictly prohibited by policy, but a review of their risk management system shows that it has a designated speculative book. How does that work? Would a large speculative loss bring smiles to the faces of the board or investment community? The answer is clearly,"No."

Addressing Governance

How is the organization governed? It is important that every employee understands how their company is managed. It usually begins with the board of directors. What is their role? What about the roles, if any, of the committees of the board like the executive and audit? What role does senior management play? Is there involvement of a risk committee or executive committee within the organization? Who participates on the risk committee? Where does the commercial management team fit in? That hierarchy should be defined and understood by the reader.

Making Policy Statements

As managers of an enterprise, there are messages that need to be emphasized over and over again. Some of these have significant implications and are important to the organization. The creation of a comprehensive policy can provide one more stage for management to reinforce important corporate issues. The inclusion of statements supporting ethical behavior, direct linkage with the Code of Conduct, the company's other ethics policies, the requirement to comply with all laws and regulations have a place in a well constructed policy. The establishment of consequences for non-compliance with policy needs to be emphatically stated. Their inclusion reiterates management's and the board's support of the concepts and how seriously they take them. It is not inappropriate to include other important concepts such as company values and some of the "softer" issues. This is an opportunity to communicate important issues to employees.

Incorporating Organizational Design

What does the organization look like? What span of control and segregation of duties have been put in place? Do we want a sales representative invoicing customers and making general ledger entries? Of course not. No matter what industry you are in, there are basic controls necessary to support the integrity of the business. This needs to be understood by employees of the company and the implementation of a proper organizational design is critical to those third parties that opine to the health of the organization like external auditors and rating agencies to name a few interested groups. The use of organizational charts and broad classifications of certain functionality with supporting narrative is helpful to instruct the reader on this critical component of the control infrastructure.

Defining Roles and Responsibilities

If the policy is properly designed and written, the reader will understand the strategy, governance and the organizational design of the company. Does it answer the question, "What is their role and responsibility with respect to the company's commercial activity?" If the policy is thorough, that question should be made abundantly clear. The establishment of a section that details the roles and responsibilities of individuals and departments/functions provides clarity to that often asked question. There are many positives to be achieved if done correctly, like developing a higher degree of employee accountability and demonstrating the role an individual(s) and department/function plays in context of overall commercial operations.

Establishing Controls and Limitations

What are the parameters we are putting around the business? This can be a simple as the inclusion of a delegation of authority or as complex as some of the multiple controls that have historically been applied to energy merchant organizations. What ever information resides here must be consistent with the board's understanding of the business parameters and the company's strategy. For the reader, this information can further define what they can and cannot do and contribute to their understanding of how the business operates. These controls should reflect the current environment the company is operating in and incorporate any new developments not accommodated for in earlier versions of the policy.

Including Other Topics

Approaching policy development from a comprehensive perspective allows for the transmittal of great deal of pertinent information. While the document itself is an establishment of major "policies" with respect to commercial operations, it is also an educational document where the addition of incremental information can further the knowledge of the various groups that are party to the policy. For example, there may be terms and definitions that are particular to the business that people in accounting would not be familiar with and the inclusion of a terms and definitions sections could be very helpful in advancing their understanding and perhaps improve communications with the commercial side of the business. There is significant opportunity for creativity here.

Conclusion

The work involved in the development of "best practice" commercial policies probably rates pretty low on most people's excitement scale. However, the value to be gained by doing so far outweighs the commitment of time necessary to accomplish the task. There is no question that in the post Enron era that companies and their boards are being held to higher standards on many levels. That certainly has been demonstrated by the implementation of Sarbanes-Oxley and the renewed focus on risk management exemplified by the COSO recommendations on Enterprise Risk Management (ERM). Proper policy formulation contributes to good governance and is just another way to execute our fiduciary responsibility to our organization's various stakeholders. The creation of commercial policies that are relevant, living, breathing documents become the cornerstone of a control infrastructure. There are excellent benchmarks available to practitioners to establish "best practice" standards in the different policy subject matter discussed above. Policies aligned with the company's strategy, processing a creative structure specifically designed to facilitate the execution of that strategy, helps enhance the organization's ability to achieve its strategic objectives.

S&P RAISE THE BAR AGAIN - ENERGY FIRMS RISK MANAGEMENT PRACTICES EVALUATED

By Cal Payne,
UtiliPoint International

It was only a year ago in 2004 when Standard & Poor's challenged the energy sector with their Liquidity Survey that asked the compelling question of how much capital or cash liquidity would be required to support a company's operations if it were to lose its credit lines. Well they are back again this year with what may be an even more telling examination of the companies they rate. On October 12, 2005 S&P announced that it would incorporate into their ongoing client analysis an expanded review of energy companies' risk management practices, raising the bar once again in what appears to be an ambitious effort to increase the depth and quality of analysis specific to the management of risk that goes into the rating process.

This exercise will present new challenges for both S&P and the companies they rate. Unlike S&P's prior liquidity survey, where their analysis was based on a formula that was universally applied, the latest set of questions asked will be subject to interpretation and so will the answers given. Rather than a relatively simple transparent quantitative outcome, a much more involved combination of quantitative and primarily qualitative analysis will have to take place and with it will come all the challenges that process represents.

Utilizing the PIM Approach

The approach that S&P is utilizing is derived from the methodology used in their evaluation of the risk management practices in the financial institutions sector. The questions developed in this new initiative focus on three broad categories:- policy, infrastructure, and methodology.

Policy

S&P asks specific questions have been formulated to determine a firm's risk culture and risk management infrastructure. A portion of the analysis focuses on a company's business strategy, its risk appetite, delegated authorities, disclosures with respect to risk, and how risk issues are communicated internally and externally.

Many of these questions will be directed at the CEO, CFO and CRO level of each respective organization. They will be listening to hear a clear articulation of strategy, and a demonstration of how the "established" risk tolerance is linked and consistent with that strategy. This series of queries will delve into how risk tolerances are established, how they are identified and prioritized, how they are managed, as well as how business

unit(s) communicate their performance towards strategic objectives while operating within a stated risk tolerance. The answers to many of the questions will come from personnel throughout the organization but the inclusion of top officer interviews in this process is telling.

I believe S&P is being deliberate here, putting at least two important concepts into play. The first is supportive of a fundamental best practice concept related to the absolute requirement for senior management to understand and approve business unit strategies. Central to that under-standing is that they should be fully aware of associated risks assumed with the execution of the strategy and that they have established risk parameters to support its implementation. Those risk parameters should be within the company's overall risk tolerance. We are speaking to the fundamental concept of good governance here. How engaged is senior management in the risk management process? What is their understanding of how those risks are being managed? What methodology was applied to determine the company's risk tolerance and how is it expressed? How are risk management related issues being communicated to the upper levels of management and the Board? What are the frequency, content, and form of those communications?

The second concept may be even more telling where the questions posed address some of the issues related to emerging best practice ERM (enterprise risk management) concepts exemplified by initiatives like COSO's (Committee of Sponsoring Organizations of the Treadway Commission) ERM Framework. In trying to ascertain the top risks a firm faces and their prioritization, S&P is looking for evidence of a process where risks are identified, assessed, and then prioritized to be managed within established corporate risk tolerances. A company who has a formalized ERM program is making a substantive statement on how serious they are with respect to the management of risk within their organi-zation.

Infrastructure

Infrastructure focuses on three main components of an organization's "infrastructure." One of which is a review of the processes typically associated with middle and back office operations. Key to this analysis is the effectiveness of the processes surrounding deal/risk capture and portfolio valuation. Is the staff in place adequate to execute the many control type functions typical to a best practice control environment? Do they have the appropriate skills? Have they been empowered and resourced to effectively do their jobs? Are they truly independent of the groups that create the risks to be managed? There are many critical control processes performed by mid and back office staff that are essential to the control infrastructure. Any weakness here undermines the integrity of the system, creating a potential for a breakdown in control that could translate into a financial loss for the company.

Are the risk management policies, processes, procedures and systems part of the internal audit group's audit planning? An aggressive audit plan can go a long way to help ensure the integrity of the infrastructure in place and help correct any deficiencies or detect structural weaknesses identified during reviews. The findings of a robust, risk based audit plan should be widely communicated throughout the various levels of management and the Audit Committee of the BOD helping to strengthen the information flow to the Board with respect to risk issues.

The next area of concern is the information technology and systems that support the company's commercial endeavors. In order to manage risk effectively, you must first capture and evaluate it. Strong risk management systems are critical to manage risk as well as preserving and optimizing value for the organization. That system must provide timely and accurate data that feeds other mission critical systems like accounting, credit risk management and operations. What is the level of investment in these systems today? Are there even systems in place? What is the backup to these systems? Is there a disaster recovery plan and has it been tested? Effective systems are enablers to the execution of strategy and critical to the effective management of risk. Appropriate investments in systems are an indicator of how robust or serious a company's risk management program is.

The last component of infrastructure is related to the quality of the training and education associated with risk management for the firm. Are there on going training programs internally? Does the company send staff to outside educational courses, seminars or conferences? What is the educational background of existing staff and their experience levels? A commitment to staff education is another strong indication of a company's commitment to effective risk management.

Methodology

Like the infrastructure analysis, the methodology section touches on multiple areas of concern. First off is risk capture and measurement. Typically, Value at Risk or VaR has been the methodology of choice to measure and control market risk. VaR has long been considered a best practice standard for risk measurement in the financial institutions sector and has been adapted for application to the energy business. What VaR methodology is applied (there are several)? How is it applied to the company's portfolios? Is the limit consistent with the company's risk tolerance? While VaR is often considered the best method to measure risk, there are other controls and limitations that can enhance the control environment or serve as the primary controls absent a VaR calculation. Examples of these are Earnings at Risk and Cash Flow at Risk analysis. What is the best approach will be a function of multiple factors related to the size and type of business being evaluated.

How is capital attributed to a company's commercial operations? Is VaR, the proxy measurement for the capital deployed towards achievement of the strategy? Is there any allocation of capital attributed to the business in the form of risk capital and/or credit related demands on capital? What are the return expectations?

In addition to VaR and other measures, a firm's ability to apply stress testing or PFE (potential future exposure) and scenario analysis to its portfolios is another important touch point in assessing a company's capabilities. Having the ability to stress portfolios and assess PFE as a regular part of managing/evaluating risk will be viewed positively. How are models created? Are they back tested? Are they independently reviewed/tested prior to adoption? Where does model development reside? Credit risk management capabilities are also part of the evaluation. The ability of a firm to accurately measure this risk by understanding the contractual rights embedded in their counterparty contracts is essential to effectively manage that risk. What is the makeup of the credit risk portfolio? Is the portfolio stressed to determine potential exposures?

Some Challenges

The foundation for best practice risk management for energy companies is essentially based on those found in the financial sector. Fundamental concepts like VaR, marking to market positions, policy development, segregation of duties, span of control protections, independence of control functions (to name a few) have come from financial institution practices.

On that basis, S&P's application of PIM for their analysis can be readily supported. However, there are some substantive differences between the financial institutions and energy companies that must be addressed.

Think of the markets that financial institutions are typically participating in; e.g. interest rates, foreign currencies, equities and fixed income securities. In general, these are very liquid and transparent markets. Depending on a financial institution's strategy, some will have the challenge of properly capturing, evaluating and accounting for derivatives that are proprietary, illiquid and outside of the box but, for the most part, the majority of their portfolios are managed in an environment where transactions are plentiful and pricing is clearly established. Where is the basis risk in U.S. currencies? There certainly is basis risk in the gas market that energy companies must deal with. Do they have physical assets to capture in their books? How about index pricing? Do they have long-term transportation agreements or storage positions to capture in their book? Unless they are new to the physical commodities business they do not have those issues to deal with. These are just some of the less than subtle differences that S&P must be sensitive to as they begin to evaluate companies.

Another of those differences is related to how you define operational risk. In financial institutions, the emphasis is typically on employee wrongdoing, the classic rogue trader example. In the energy sector that issue must be dealt with, but what about the impact of a failure to make a pipeline nomination? What is the impact of a plant that cannot be dispatched due to a maintenance problem? What happens when you lose supply that supports your ongoing obligations in a rising price environment? That feels like operational risk to me. So how are we defining operational risk and is it consistent with the evaluation metrics of financial institutions?

When looking at risk measurement methodologies like VaR, considerable thought will have to be invested in understanding what that number represents and how effective is it as a control. Does their VaR calculation include asset positions? If for example, the asset in question is an unsold merchant plant, is 20 years of capacity captured? Does that number clarify the risk or does it distort embedded risk in the aggregate portfolio? Are there transactions outside of the VaR calculation? Is the VaR methodology employed the best for the nature of that business? Who can make that determination, S&P? What about transmission and pipeline transportation contracts? Are they in there? This is just one issue that will be difficult to qualify and could be a point of disagreement.

While there are different strategies in the financial institutions group, they are more narrowly defined than in energy. This process of evaluating risk management practices cannot be a one size fits all approach. There will be many differentiating factors that must be taken into consideration when analyzing survey responses. Among these are what is the underlying business. Is it a utility, a producer, or a fully integrated major like Exxon? Is it an aggregator, a merchant trader, a transportation company and so on? What is their stated strategy? What is the size of the business? All these factors will have to be taken into consideration when determining the relative strength of a company's risk management program. An important question that remains to be answered is, does S&P have the requisite expertise to effectively make those qualitative determinations?

A real challenge may be more basic that the issues detailed above. Will companies be totally honest when responding to the questionnaires and interviews? I have always been sympathetic to the rating agencies, equity and fixed income analysts who have to rely on what companies say they are doing. No one really wants to admit there may be some weakness in how they conduct their business. Manage our risk? You bet we do. The truth is that there can be large variances between what we say, and actually do. S&P's approach here is far more invasive (in a positive way) that seeks to see an actual demonstration of what is represented instead of just relying on the statements of others.

Conclusion

This certainly is an ambitious program. To respond appropriately will require careful thought and preparation by the companies surveyed. Once the information is generated there will be a tremendous amount of valuable data to evaluate. Standard and Poor's effort here is applaudable. Any attempt to better understand in-depth the capability of rated companies is better for the investment community that takes comfort in the ratings generated. Their challenge will be to recognize the unique characteristics of the energy sector and of the companies occupying that space. To that end they have already solicited input from industry practitioners to better understand the issues. It appears that the analysts at S&P are taking the necessary steps to bring their capabilities up to speed to guarantee a quality end product. S&P is riding the crest of what is an emerging issue that reinforces the concept that companies have a fiduciary responsibility to manage the risks that their enterprise face. The days of giving lip service to such an important issue is over and a company's ability to effectively manage risk can now affect how its credit worthiness will be rated.

THE NEW CREDIT PARADIGM: A CASE STUDY

By Cal Payne,
UtiliPoint International

Last week the International Energy Credit Association held its 81st annual meeting in Carlsbad, California offering energy sector credit professionals the opportunity to network and attend educational sessions on current and emerging issues important to their effective management of credit risk. So what, who cares? Credit is just credit, right? Assign a credit line and collect receivables. That is credit risk management. Or is it? Just think for a moment, in the overall scheme of things, if there is one risk that is common to all companies, that risk is credit and its impact can be substantive. If there ever was a risk that should be managed on an enterprise wide basis, that risk is credit. The role of credit in an organization should not be restricted to just the reduction in credit related losses. Effective credit risk management can and should impact organizations in much broader, substantial ways. To do so requires a change in methodology, a shift to what I am calling the new credit paradigm, a robust, multifaceted and comprehensive approach to the management of credit risk. What follows is an example of some of the changes one client's credit group implemented to make that shift.

Credit's Contingent Call on Capital

I think it was Jeff Skilling that said Enron's problems could essentially be distilled down to a run on the bank. While that certainly is an understatement, there is more that some element of truth in that comment. The contingent call on capital associated with their huge physical and financial commodity business drained the organization of its liquidity resources as negative news emerged and their credit rating deteriorated forcing them to seek bankruptcy protection. Others in the industry faced similar scenarios as the rating agencies began the wholesale downgrading of credit ratings in the sector. It is important that a credit group be as much aware of the credit that they have received from others as they are of the credit they have extended. The leadership of this company's credit group recognized that they needed to look at the mirror image of credit as critical to understanding the potential impact of reductions in counterparty credit capacity due to any individual or combination of market or credit events (e.g. a credit downgrade). Quantifying the impact of credit type events on their own organization by understanding in detail, the credit capacity that had been extended to them, allowed them to manage that potential impact within the company's financial means averting a crisis.

Creating Credit Capacity

In most credit organizations, the focus is on credit extension to the company's various counterparties. The lines created should be consistent with what the credit analysis supports and the business requirements of the firm. Another concept that is equally important is the need to help a firm gain credit capacity extended from others that helps it facilitate the execution of their strategy. In this case, there was a substantial need for more capacity, so the credit group worked with other credit departments to increase lines or establish new ones. The proactive advancement of the company's story to targeted counterparties through mailings, meetings, formal presentations and consistent networking allowed my client to get capacity consistent with their business objectives. Counterparties that were targeted for such efforts were determined by working with the commercial people to identify the most commercially desirable companies to work with.

Vendor Qualification

During an early conversation with the CFO of the company we discussed the credit risk associated with day to day purchasing activity. To my surprise, he said how can you have risk when you are the one paying the bill? In any business that risk is mark-to-market exposure. If a company is in the commodity business (and this one is) and buys at a fixed price in a rising market from a supplier who fails to deliver, guess what, that company will be in the market purchasing at a higher price then original contracted rate. That differential is their mark-to-market exposure and essentially represents a credit loss to that company. If a firm awards a contract to a supplier for the installation of a communications system and that supplier goes bankrupt and cannot perform, the purchaser's only option is to go to the next higher bidder and hope they are willing to contract with them. That difference in cost is a proxy for what could be deemed as the mark-to-market impact of the initial supplier's default. Clearly there is a potential exposure every time you make a purchase and the need to manage that risk or qualify that risk should fall to a credit professional. The bottom line is there is credit risk on both the receivable and payable side of the ledger. That was an expansion in scope they accepted early on.

Managing Credit as a Portfolio

Like any book of business, the aggregation of sales and purchases creates a portfolio. The same is true in credit where the same transactions represent credit risk that must be managed. The portfolio concept was embraced by the credit group who took the necessary steps to implement the idea. The first task was to recognize that to effectively manage any portfolio; you need to first capture the transactions in a meaningful way to provide the necessary data. Once they accurately captured the "book," the credit department made it a priority to understand that portfolio in detail. How exposures to or from a counterparty change overtime, what offsets may exist within a relationship and what is the makeup of the portfolio in terms of credit quality are just some of the information they consider when managing credit risk on a portfolio basis.

They had established benchmarks that answered questions like; does the book reflect the level of risk consistent with our established risk appetite (that appetite should be clearly established)? What are my credit quality goals? Are we biased towards single "A's", or do we want to emphasis "BBB's"? Do we want a component of below investment grade credits in the book? Do we want to consciously diversify the portfolio by targeting multiple industries? The credit portfolio was then further controlled on a more granular basis by placing durational, concentration and temporal limits on individual credits or segments of the book. Credit risk was additionally managed by the execution of targeted transacting with specific counterparties or other segments of the portfolio. You cannot do that if you do not understand your book.

Credit Analysis

If a company intends to extend credit to a customer, there should be a basis for that decision supported by some form of analysis. Depending of the size of the customer, different approaches are warranted. A multi page analysis is not required for a utility residential customer, but a large dollar commercial/industrial customer merits more than just a cursory review. Some credit people still look at a percentage of net worth as the basis for establishing a line along with a few calculations of certain ratios. This credit shop's approach evolved to where they look at a credit in a similar way a commercial bank, rating agency or fixed income investor does. Analysis now includes the generation of multiple ratios targeting different components of the company's underlying financial strength. Comparing year on year results helps to determine trends both positive and negative.

This organization's credit people now differentiate between industry segments. A bank is not an industrial customer. An energy merchant is not a government agency and so on. For publicly traded companies, a thorough reading of SEC filings and understanding of the notes to financial statements are great aids to understanding a credit. What are their contingent liabilities? Is there a shift in strategy? Their credit analysts understand their counterparties in far greater detail and the decision making regarding those companies is based on a more robust, thorough analysis.

Facilitating vs. Encumbering

The easiest answer for a credit professional to give when faced with a credit decision is to say no to a transaction or the establishment of a line of credit. You can't have a credit loss if you do not extend a credit line. It is easy to do and does not require a huge investment of time or the application of any level of creativity. This company challenged its credit department to find ways to facilitate transactions and or establish credit relationships. To do so requires a level of creativity where people are encouraged to think outside of the box to solve a problem credit issue, helping the commercial side of the business achieve its strategic objectives. The ability to properly structure a deal to afford the protection the company needs while allowing the transaction to progress helps move the company forward. Credit is now working with the commercial side in a healthy partnership rather than interacting exclusively as a support and control function.

Applying Available Tools to Mitigate Risk

There are many ways to protect an organization or enhance its position with respect to the management of credit risk outside of a secured transaction. The application of these tools supports several of the issues highlighted above. The establishment of contractual rights or creative structuring of an agreement can help close a transaction with a weak credit that might not get done otherwise. The addition of master netting arrangements (allowing companies to net payables and receivables between specific legal entities and in some cases across multiple commodities) and establishing rights of offset certainly can be used to reduce credit risk and potential demands on liquidity. The active support and promotion of physical clearing solutions as efficient ways of mitigating risk and addressing liquidity issues are another valuable tool. The establishment of margining rights and the aggressive management of margin arrangements also work well to maximize cash flow and bracket credit risk. All of these avenues were pursued on a consistent basis.

Conclusion

The change in the objectives of this company's credit group was dramatic and redefined their ongoing contribution to their firm. It altered they way they were perceived by senior management, internal clients and the organizations they dealt with externally. What occurred was an evolution in approach and a broadening of their scope of operation that moved them from simply being a credit function to becoming an effective credit risk management organization. Some of the components of that shift are summarized below:

- From performing simple credit analysis to the initiation of a more sophisticated bank like approach to analyzing a counterparty.

- From looking at the credit worthiness of their customers only to include vendor/supplier qualification managing both the asset and liability.

- From credit line extension only to include creating credit capacity consistent with their company's strategy.

- From acting primarily as a control function to include becoming a facilitator embracing the concept of finding creative ways to get transactions done in partnership with the commercial side of the business.

- From being unaware of the cash and liquidity impact of credit to actively working to minimize demands on liquidity and maximizing cash flow.

- From looking at credit on a counterparty by counterparty basis to include an emphasis on portfolio management with specific credit quality goals and objectives.

- From being reactive in approach to issues to being proactive and out ahead of issues and initiatives.

- From working to eliminate any credit loss to embracing the concepts that some credit losses within a pre established loss appetite may be the better answer.

The answer to the question regarding who cares about a bunch of industry credit practitioners getting together for their annual meeting is anyone in management who understands the impact of an effective credit risk management program. Those who understand should be encouraged that a group of people whose daily work has a growing importance to their respective organizations is meeting, exchanging ideas, building business and personal relationships and learning about current issues and new concepts that will help them to challenge convention and move in the direction of the new credit paradigm.

HEDGING 360: THE CASE FOR IMPROVED PERSPECTIVES AMONG RISK MANAGEMENT PARTICIPANTS IN THE REGULATED ENERGY UTILITY INDUSTRY

By Leigh Parkinson,
Energy Consultant,
RiskAdvisory (A Division of SAS)

Four years after the wholesale marketing and trading sector meltdown, utility hedging is once again seen as a vital tool for the management of financial and commodity risks. Many utility companies have attempted to compete in the marketplace by enhancing corporate performance through the creation of unregulated subsidiaries to capitalize on perceived opportunities. These unregulated trading activities inevitably lead to areas of conflict or perceived conflict between these subsidiaries and the core regulated utility business. To a large degree it would now appear that utilities have abandoned these initiatives and that hedging activities are relegated to managing rate volatility on behalf of companies' constituent customers.

Our research indicates that the industry is more comfortable with the use of hedging in this capacity today. Indeed, across the entire spectrum of industry influencers – utility companies, regulators and consumer advocates – all seem to be assigning and assuming roles and responsibilities to employ common-sense hedging strategies. The industry is in broad agreement that practical uses of hedging techniques can help to create price stability for consumers, manage the balance sheet and avoid speculation. Our research would further indicate that there is evidence of increased cooperation and collaboration between those previously adversarial groups. This spirit of cooperation should provide significant cost reductions in the regulatory process and ultimately benefit consumers, if this trend continues.

This rosy picture is very likely influenced by the current high commodity price environment where almost any magnitude of hedging that was undertaken early in 2005 would have validated this new spirit of collaboration to all the parties who recommend, approve and manage policies for risk management decision making in the utility world. In the realm of utility public opinion right now, hedging is a good thing. Our research indicates that, at this juncture, hedging is widely regarded as an efficient tool, and that perceptions have grown more favorable this year relative to results from research we conducted a year ago. Last year's hedging looks smart, protecting consumers from historically high volatility and prices for energy fuel supplies and, not surprisingly, the degree of acrimony between regulators, utilities and consumer groups has diminished where common sense hedging was employed.

But the true test for the longevity of this collaborative spirit is still ahead. Commodity prices have cyclical up and down trends. Mathematical theory would suggest that even at these high fuel price levels there still exists an even possibility – like a flip of the coin – that prices could continue higher or reverse the current rising trend. It will become increasingly difficult to enter into new hedging strategies if price s continue ever higher with the risk being, of course, that the collaborators decide that hedging should be constrained and prices continue to rise leaving ratepayers exposed with fewer hedges in place. The larger risk to the current state of calm is a cyclical price decline if significant hedges are still in place. Such a decline would prevent consumers from participating in a lower price environment. In the past this has ignited ominous second-guessing: regulators and consumer advocates become Monday morning quarterbacks, suggesting that utility management should have foreseen the drop and allowed customers to participate in the downward movement. Essentially this viewpoint asks the impossible: Why could mainstream utility management not do what only a handful of traders were able to do; beat the market? It's almost the same as saying: Why didn't everyone win on their trip to Vegas?

Our supposition is simple: the utility industry now has a historic opportunity to use the current environment to correct some serious ineffi-ciencies of the past, especially with regards to setting expectations in a rate-setting process that begins with – and sets the structure for – future hedging decisions. The utility industry can demonstrate both responsibility and innovation in this historic moment by changing the backward-looking nature of the rate-setting process, embracing techniques of mechanistic hedging and minding the details of its business through comprehensive monitoring of market positions and measuring and managing the risk and credit exposures endemic to commodity volatility.

Impossible, you say? Au contraire. The willingness to better the rate setting process exists among all participants, today. Research and development advancements in powerful new software indicate that all this is possible and within the industry's grasp.

Times are Changing

In the past, when utilities have wrongly divined the price, it has been easy for regulatory bodies to look backwards and point the finger at the utility, charging that management should have known better. A utility's primary role should be to ensure a secure supply of energy and delivery to its constituents. Utilities do not have the ability and compensation incentives to foster an environment to employ trading personnel that are capable of picking market direction correctly and are never compensated for attempting to do so. To a large degree, utilities have put themselves in this uncomfortable regulatory position by sticking their necks out on behalf of the consumers and assuming the role of price forecaster. If a utility does occasionally make the correct call on price direction, all the financial benefit for that decision will flow through to the ratepayers and if the utility gets it wrong they run the risk of material regulatory disallowances. The rate-setting process practically institutionalizes a structure that fosters animosity and contentiousness. The net effect of this acrimonious relationship between a utility and its regulator has caused tremendous wastes of time and money at lengthy rate hearings with escalating emotion and tension on all sides.

For the last two years, RiskAdvisory has administered spot polls of attendees at the Utility Risk Management Summit Conferences we host in Chicago. The results are inevitably skewed toward the utilities' point of view because more of their representatives attend than do people from regulatory or consumer advocate groups. Nonetheless, the accumulation of data in 2004 and 2005 enables both year-over-year comparisons and initial trend analysis. References to industry sentiment also are derived from these surveys. The full results are available on www.RiskAdvisory.com.

The 2005 survey revealed some interesting changes from the prior year and they have most likely been caused by the rapidly escalating price environment. First, there's a definite desire for more collaborative approaches for managing ratepayer risk among all the groups involved in the rate-setting process. Of course, sharp natural gas price increases in 2005 and 2006 will likely represent seminal years because of the sheer number of North American rate cases convened. Those cases are mostly reactive, with utilities needing to hike prices in response to commodity volatility and upward cost pressures and every utility feels pain when there are the inevitable disallowances.

But in 2005, research indicates that survey respondents believe utilities, regulators and consumer advocacy groups can employ more productive methods for coming to a consensus on rates. The landscape seems to be shifting, however gradually, because there is a growing realization that there is a better way. Nearly 70 percent of respondents to our 2005 survey believed that regulators, consumer advocates, direct marketers and utilities can come to terms on hedging programs before they are implemented. They can work through some negotiation processes to agree on a percentage of a portfolio that should be fixed on the consumers' behalf, based on a perception of ratepayers' appetite for volatility in their utility bills. The theory is that, by using this upfront approach, the utility's sole responsibility beyond its involvement and input into the collaborative process is the implementation of the agreed upon risk management program.

If future pass-through adjustments are needed because actual costs exceeded forecasts, then everyone shares some responsibility for the "decisions," on behalf of ratepayers and allowances are made because a measure of consensus was achieved on guidelines at the beginning of the process. Assuming a utility implements the program according to the consensus plan, it should be absolved from any responsibility of forecasting which way prices are headed and then trying to hedge appropriately. Animosity and contention should, in this approach, be reduced or removed from the regulatory risk equation. Consequently the industry's current – and correct – sense that rate hearings are costly and ineffective could be reversed.

Meanwhile many rate case hearings linger on in their traditionally acrimonious mode, in large part because utilities have continued to put themselves in the impossible position of predicting price direction on behalf of the ratepayer and as often as not, getting it wrong. We contend that this is precisely the area where the utilities can make life easier for themselves, the regulators and consumer advocacy groups. Utilities should consider adopting a mechanistic hedging program that eliminates the quasi-speculative aura that sometimes surrounds hedging decisions. When the utility systematically fixes the agreed percentage of the portfolio – at a pre-ordained time, without consideration for market and price activity – then they are implementing a mechanistic program that reduces the perception of opportunism and speculation. Even if all utilities cannot get comfortable with immediately adopting and implementing a mechanistic hedging approach, the utilities in our survey overwhelmingly indicated that they want regulators' blessing for the design of their hedging programs. While utilities aren't always convinced of the regulators' ability to comprehend and distinguish the nitty-gritty details of a hedging program, they still welcome the concept of an ex ante agreement on the parameters and guidelines of such a program. Mechanistic programs can incorporate industry knowledge, financial best practices and balance constituent interests that are agreeable to all parties and represent the best interests of the ratepayer.

If mechanistic hedging is being considered, the difficulty then becomes the determination of the ratepayers' appetite for risk. Consumers are not homogenous and risk appetites will be very diverse. How much price exposure are consumers willing to absorb if a utility is fully exposed, in exchange for participation in a possible downward move in prices? How much of a premium over market prices would consumers pay to ensure they were not exposed to prices above a predetermined level? The questions are many and there is no easy solution. More and more utilities are engaging market research firms to define how much volatility various ratepayer classes – commercial, industrial and retail – are willing to tolerate in a fluctuating commodity environment. Focus groups are polled to get a sense of the risk profile of this diverse customer base. This research – and a commitment to educating the public about hedging and its impact on utility bills – creates a more collaborative foundation for rate-setting hearings. Theoretically, the hearings should become less contentious and even more productive for the participating groups because they are giving the public what it wants: increased transparency, pre-dictability and cooperation. The utility no longer has to stick out their neck … as much.

Minding the Store

As we've discussed above, regulatory risk could be more manageable than has been the case in the past. There is evidence of a willing spirit now in the industry to change the way that risk responsibility is assigned and rates set.

Yet even while energy market participants face the challenges posed by the need to manage their exposures to commodity prices, other risks remain. Companies face a number of internal risks in a volatile commodity environment. Interest rates, foreign exchange rates, shifting volumetric profiles, supply disruptions and credit risks all pose their challenges. Failure to properly manage these exposures can result in financial losses, credit downgrades, regulatory disallowances and the erosion of shareholder value and investor confidence. Ignoring these challenges puts the utility at risk of abrogating its end of the operational agreements that rate payers and regulators expect, in turn creating a return to the contentious rate-setting environment the utility seeks to avoid.

Utility companies can mitigate this pervasive uncertainty by having at their fingertips accurate and timely information available on all relevant risks. Companies can control and optimize the complex risk profiles associated with their involvement in energy markets, but they can only do so through robust information technology and software systems. Deciding what those systems should do will determine whether the utility operates at its absolute best when facing these challenges.

The software solutions required by today's energy market participants must be evaluated for their ability to measure the value and risk in the portfolio of commodity exposures, ensure data integrity, reduce the risk of error in portfolio-tracking models, account for real options in the asset portfolio and help companies model the volumetric risk in their commodity positions. Other considerations include capabilities for multi-commodity support (electricity, fuels and natural gas); deal capture on web-enabled software; multiple financial transaction types (physical spot, forward contracts, futures, options and swaps); multiple energy market transactions (transmission/transportation, power generators, power load, FX swaps and inter-book transactions); and, graphical presentation of earnings distribution. Most importantly, all of this information must be accessed and presented in a way that allows both information and analysis to be delivered to senior management in a timely and instructive manner.

In addition to accounting for all the financial products listed above, options have become a large part of energy firms' portfolio management strategy. Any trading/risk management system needs to properly value and assess the non-linear risk of a portfolio that contains options or more complex agreements that have embedded optionality within them. Equally important is the ability to run multiple scenarios quickly while capturing this non-linearity so firms can properly understand how its policies may affect both financial and physical exposures. In combination with an environment that can quantify credit risk, utilizing the same underlying data, the user will be fully empowered to understand how any market event will impact the firm, with regards to price, volumetric and credit risks.

In conclusion, RiskAdvisory believes that today's utilities have the means and the momentum to change for the better both the way they manage external political risks and the manner in which they monitor the operations of their internal financial transactions. The question today is whether there is the will to change. The events that triggered change in 2001, and the prevailing outlook for continuing volatility, indicate that change will be a necessity in the utility industry going forward and it's comforting to know that managing the shape of future change is at the fingertips of industry executives.

THE CCRO AND IT'S IMPACT

By Dr. Gary M. Vasey
UtiliPoint International, Inc.

One potential indicator of increasing industry maturity is the emergence of standards and best practice and a most important example of this is the work undertaken by the Committee of Chief Risk Officers (CCRO). The CCRO was formed by a group of Chief Risk Officers representing a variety of energy industry firms to develop a comprehensive set of risk management best practices for all energy trading firms whether merchant or regulated utility. The CCRO has issued a set of formal papers covering areas such as risk management disclosures, credit risk management, valuation and risk metrics and organizational and independence that are being closely scrutinized by industry participants including federal agencies such as the SEC, FERC, NEMA etc.

Why Is CCRO Important?

Without a doubt, the CCRO activities and recommendations is one of the single most important initiatives at work in the energy business today and will have far reaching and hopefully positive implications for energy trading through the next decade. It was the lack of formal standards and a lack of understanding of business practices in general that contributed to the serious issues surrounding the merchant sector this last year and also contributed to previous crises in the business such as the California situation, price spikes and credit issues. Each crisis faced by the industry has brought with it a renewed emphasis on an aspect of risk management whether that is credit risk exposure or the need for Value at Risk (VaR) and similar measures for valuation purposes.

Of course, the issues that the industry must face as a result of the collapse of Enron, the demise of speculative trading and the merchant sector in general are much more serious than any that came before. The issue is one of believability and credibility with shareholders, counterparty's and analysts. It is now about visibility internally and externally into the balance sheet. To get past these issues, the 'public' has to have confidence in the numbers and that means that the numbers must have been generated in a standard way according to generally understood criteria. In other words – a standard approach is required.

There are many other reasons why the CCRO recommendations are likely to be taken up by the industry outside of restoring confidence in energy trading firms. Just as VaR became a standard methodology (at least in name) across the industry as a result of pressure on company directors from outside auditors, so the new standards provide the energy auditing firms a way to restore their own lost credibility. It was partly the outside auditors' ability to help 'fudge' company results in the absence of true standards for valuation and disclosure in the energy trading business that contributed to the crisis of 2001. They, as much as any party involved, will seek the safety and security of standards for their own future reputations. Just as the Capital Adequacy Standards of the 1998 Basel Accord changed everything in the financial sector, so will the CCRO recommendations impact the energy markets.

What Is The Next Step?

As the expectation of industry uptake of the standards increases in magnitude and need, energy firms must undertake a serious review of the standards and their own business practices to compare one with the other. Essentially, the energy firms need to perform a gap analysis to assess where they fall short of meeting the standards. Once this has been established, new procedures, business rules and methods must be introduced to close the compliance gap.

Underpinning the implementation of new methods, business practices and rules are the systems utilized to perform transaction management and risk management and once the gap analysis has been performed, these systems will also need to be audited to ensure that they can provide the functionality required to support a CCRO compliant business model. Many of the vendors are now also reviewing the CCRO recommendations and establishing what modifications they will be required to make to their systems to allow customer compliance.

The time to start this process is now. As industry and outside industry pressure for the adoption of the standards increases, so will the urgency for energy firms to implement them. The first step in that process is to perform a gap analysis and utilize that analysis to build an implementation project plan. Energy firms cannot afford to lag behind peers when credibility with shareholders is at stake.

ETRM SOFTWARE AS AN ESSENTIAL PART OF RISK MANAGEMENT POLICY

By Dr. Gary M. Vasey,
UtiliPoint International, Inc.

In the era of Sarbanes-Oxley and with the industry making recommendations on risk management through the CCRO, the management of enterprise risk and emphasis on corporate governance means that proper management of the business process around energy trading are a significant component in overall risk management. Not only do trades and their associated transactions have to be properly recorded but there has to be an audit trail of all changes made to that data along with a record of workflow. As the ETRM system becomes the 'system of record' for much of the trading data, security of access to data and functions also needs to be guaranteed by the software. Today, evidence suggests that many companies still over rely on spreadsheets1 that are open to abuse, error and oversight.

To comply with properly drawn up risk management procedures as well as to comply with corporate governance mandates, companies trading energy must have a comprehensive ETRM system in place that provides surety and auditability. Additionally, they must have access to proper functionality; functionality that actually supports their business and business processes. This includes adequate reporting tools and the ability to drill down into data intelligently to account for variances, to properly explain results and to mine for trends that can be used to set up strategies.

Today, ETRM software as provided by vendors is approaching this level of requirement and only an ETRM software solution can provide the basis for complying with internal and external risk policies. Even if imperfect, it is better than the ubiquitous spreadsheets.

Risk Management Tools and Methods

Many of the risk management software packages and toolsets were originally developed for the financial industry and as a result do not always reflect the complexity of the energy business. Most energy oriented risk systems will perform Value at Risk and Mark to Market calculations and some will also provide stress testing and Monte Carlo based VaR. Where many fall short is in dealing with the physical side of the business in terms of measuring volume and deliverability risk or modeling generation assets or storage. Too often, physical assets have to be modeled imperfectly as an option as work around for example.

However, most risk systems can perform the basics of risk management for energy and provide a level of risk reporting and, most vendors are now moving to address omissions. Despite that, the energy industry is complex and there will always be situations where proprietary models and approaches need to be taken. The quant will continue to be in demand to help set up models for complex options, real options, storage models and the like. Once again, this means that ETRM software needs to be fully integrated with proprietary or best in class risk management tools and models. The architectural movements outlined above may help in this regard.

What is important when using risk management software as part of an ETRM system is to understand just what it can and can't do. Users need to be aware of its strengths and weaknesses and build that understanding in to risk policy to ensure that the chance for mistakes and errors are minimized. Despite a 15+ year history, ETRM software is still maturing as a class of software. Recently, Many of the vendors have began to migrate their software to new architectures that provide for additional benefits for users particularly in terms of connectivity. Although imperfect, today's business and regulatory environment demands that some form of ETRM software solution is utilized since it provides some degree of control over other solutions such as spreadsheets.

To properly comply with a comprehensive risk policy, it is imperative to have some form of ETRM system in place that provides at least basic database, reporting, audit trailing and workflow. The key to success is in understanding the flaws of the ETRM system and ensuring that those flaws are compensated for in the company's risk policy and procedures. Similarly, it needs to be recognized that many energy risk management software solutions will provide only the basic risk management requirements and may need to be supplemented by work arounds and proprietary models. Again, these weaknesses need to understood and compensated for with an overall risk policy. Finally, review of ETRM systems and software should always be an important component in any risk audit undertaken.

SIX

THE IMPACT AND BENEFITS OF NEW ETRM ARCHITECTURES

By Dr. Gary M. Vasey and Andrew Bruce
UtiliPoint International, Inc.

Many ETRM vendors have migrated, or are in the process of migrating, their application architectures from a client/server model to n-tier and a service oriented architectures (SOA). Although the chosen architectures differ from vendor-to-vendor, the impact is somewhat the same. The new architectures are allowing vendors to deliver solutions that are more flexible, configurable, and scalable, while also providing significantly improved connectivity via web services for example. These new architectures are set to have a broad impact on the industry.

The IT Challenge

A sustained period of underinvestment in IT architectures and tools following the industry uncertainty created by the merchant collapse is now having its impact. Our study demonstrates that IT departments are usually relatively small and often lack the tools that would allow them to be proactive and truly engaged with the business in order to be responsive. Instead, IT staffs are often focused on holding together legacy environments, addressing data issues, dealing with vendors, and trying to keep up with the needs of the business.

Today's energy company or utility, is faced with a multitude of business challenges not the least of which is ensuring a proper response to new regulations and standards such as Sarbanes-Oxley and the CCRO recommendations. Additionally, the nature of the energy business is such that ongoing change in both regulations and standards is to be anticipated. Business strategies have to be somewhat fluid to respond to both new opportunities and challenges. But the ability of the business to respond is in large part dictated by the effectiveness of the IT department and its ability to rapidly assess requirements and deploy systems in support of the business.

The majority of power marketing functions reviewed by our research maintain a heterogeneous solution landscape that comprises a large number of different software solutions and applications to support the business (Figure 6.1). Many of these solutions remain internally developed or even spreadsheet-based and a majority still rely on the use of mainly manual interfaces between applications (Figure 6.2).

The level of complexity of these application architectures combined with the lack of IT infrastructures designed to support integration and connectivity between applications, is both surprising and concerning. The demands placed on IT departments that have to maintain a poorly integrated and heterogeneous application environment while being positioned to adequately respond to the ongoing needs of the business, are high. Similarly, the company's ability to comply with the requirements of Sarbanes-Oxley, good financial reporting, and other corporate governance requirements must be potentially compromised.

Figure 6.1: Number of applications deployed to support power marketing activities

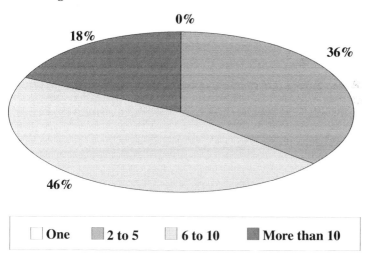

Figure 6.2 Integration levels

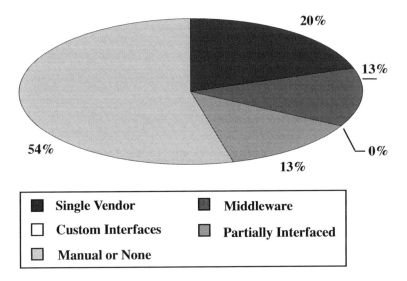

For example, as the merchant segment of the industry began to collapse, some utilities were forced to abandon plans for non-regulated merchant-like business units and all utilities dropped back to the safety of an asset-centric business strategy. Similarly, as retail deregulation stalled, utility business plans to respond to the threat of competition were sidelined and mothballed. Each time such an event occurs, the IT department's burden increases, if only temporarily. Even for a utility contemplating entering a new regional market, the IT staff may have only weeks or months to respond, providing the necessary software tools and infrastructures that will allow the business to achieve its goals in the planned timeframe.

Potential Solutions

One way for an IT department to meet the needs of the business in this type of environment is to employ seasoned staffs with both energy business and IT experience. In the study, most IT managers cited the need for experienced and knowledgeable analysts that were involved with the business on a day-to-day basis and were a party to the business decisions being made. To be properly responsive, IT needs ought to enjoy the right level of visibility at the executive level within a business that understands the true importance of IT in meeting business goals.

Additionally, IT must find ways to second guess the business by keeping track of industry change at any number of levels, from macro industry structural issues to local reporting requirements. This is in addition to maintaining an active awareness of the latest trends in hardware, software and other technologies and methodologies! Many of the IT professionals that we talked with routinely undertook "what if" planning exercises, carefully reviewing the likely impacts of certain industry or business objective changes. This approach was credited with helping quickly trigger IT initiatives to support changed business objectives.

Most cited architecture as a critical component of an IT strategy designed to deliver agility. By ensuring a relatively low cost but flexible IT infrastructure with connectivity and integration built in, new software solutions can be deployed faster and more efficiently without too much disruption to the other business processes around them. Equally, legacy applications can more easily be replaced or updated.

Much of the difficulty facing the power marketing IT department lies with the relative immaturity of commercial software solutions. Although the situation has dramatically improved in recent years, many IT departments are still grappling with yesterday's applications.

Faced with many of the same problems, vendors often have their own challenges keeping software current with respect to new requirements and in meeting the diverse requirements of different types and flavors of power marketing businesses in their client base. Additionally, vendors need to continually make new sales to maintain cash flow while keeping code line quality high.

Users also often fall behind with software upgrades. For the IT department, this issue is magnified according to the number of different solutions deployed. The IT department is faced with multiple vendors, multiple products and multiple different upgrade schema. They also have to figure out the points of integration between those solutions and between the solution set and the rest of the enterprise.

Investment in architectures to help solve the integration issues and reduce the heterogeneity of the application landscape will ease the IT burden, help make IT more responsive to the needs of the business, re-invigorate the vendor community and reduce IT costs in the longer term. While IT may be viewed as a cost center in utilities particularly, it must be recognized that investment in adaptable IT architectures is an enabler for the business.

It is readily apparent that IT resources face, and will continue to face, considerable challenges in meeting the needs of the business in a responsive and effective manner. Today, these resources are more likely to be deployed in trying to maintain a heterogeneous and poorly integrated environment than in planning ahead. In fact, they are doing both, but by virtue of the legacy environments in place they are forced to do so sub-optimally.

A New Era of ETRM Software?

The benefits for the end user and the developer of these relatively newly available architectures are substantial but perhaps, most importantly, they provide the built-in connectivity that allows the integration issues to be solved. In effect, the new architectures being deployed by the ETRM vendors provide many of the following benefits;

• Provide connectivity that allows integration with enterprise applications, external data feeds and applications and provides the basis for constructing a true best in class suite of fully integrated ETRM applications;

• Enhances scalability of the ETRM software through the easy addition of additional processing power;

• Provides the basis for the addition of workflow and business process management tools, audit and document management capabilities;

• Allows for enhanced reporting functionality via the addition of a reporting application or using the vendors own reporting capabilities. Some of the vendors are now offering drill-down reporting complete with graphing and mapping features;

• Provides the vendor the opportunity to build in more configurability allowing the package to be customized for each users particular environment and culture thereby enhancing implementation success rates and allowing the vendor to pursue a traditional software vendor business model more easily;

• Enhances the vendor's ability to keep up with industry change by allowing them to break the application up into smaller modules of more discrete functionality;

• Enhances the support and maintainability of the ETRM application.

There are many additional benefits of these architectures including the ability to build data marts and data warehouses from which to perform more analysis.

As vendors migrate their current applications to these new architectures and platforms, they will be able to serve their users with more flexible, usable and customizable but supported third-party software. However, the implication of this migration is that the dichotomy of requirements described above can be met with best in class ETRM software suites from a single or multiple vendors. The lack of integration and the risks inherent with that lack of integration seen among marketers and utilities today can potentially be resolved.

These new architectures provide users of ETRM software a number of considerable business benefits. This section reviews how users can benefit from this migration to new architectures.

Improved Ease of Use

For any user of software, usability is a key purchasing criteria. This is particularly so in the ETRM software category where the sheer complexity and volatility of the business means that almost every system implementation is in reality akin to a custom solution. But what is usability, why is it so important and how does it benefit users?

Software Usability

Software usability is a complex term that is used to describe how the software interacts efficiently with its users. Usability or 'ease of use', as a requirement of software, incorporates the following five essential characteristics; effectiveness, efficiency, engaging, error tolerant and easy to learn[4]. These five characteristics must be designed into any software at the very beginning requiring user involvement in the design process. Software that meets these characteristics and is therefore highly useable and will provide significant business benefits for both the users and the vendor. The five characteristics of software usability may be defined as follows;

Effectiveness

Effectiveness is the completeness and accuracy with which users achieve specified goals and is determined by whether the user's goals are met successfully and whether all work is correct. In the context of today's energy companies, it also includes the ability to ensure security of access and data to just those users or user roles that are authorized, the ability of

---

[4]What Does Usability Mean: Looking Beyond Ease of Use. Whitney Quesenbery, STC 2001 Conference Proceedings.

related groups of users to work together collaboratively to achieve a common business objective, and an accurate record of what was done by whom and when.

Efficiency

Efficiency is the speed, with accuracy, at which users can complete the tasks for which they use the software. Efficiency metrics include the num

ber of keystrokes required or the total time spent performing a particular action. To achieve efficiency, tasks should be defined from the user's point of view within the software.

Engaging

A user interface is engaging if it suits the user's way of looking at or entering information and it is satisfying to use. To be engaging, information must be presented in a manner consistent with the user's expectations and using language in the form of screen labels that the user is culturally familiar with. It may also involve offering the user different ways to look at data including graphical representations.

Error Tolerant

An error tolerant software system is designed to prevent errors caused by the user's interaction and to help the user recover from any errors that do occur.

Easy to Learn

An interface which is easy to learn is essential to user adoption of the system and furthermore, to their ability to extract value from the system that contributes towards return on investment for the investment. A system that is easy to learn now only provides online help but goes further in using tools to guide users through processes while providing a familiar look and feel and process flow to the user.

Ease of Use in ETRM Software

ETRM software developers face a task of great magnitude in meeting usability goals for their software. Firstly, the energy industry is, and continues to be, volatile with respect to requirements and it is subject to periodic disruptive change as a result of structural, regulatory and market driven change. Secondly, while ETRM vendors wish to provide standard software solutions to the broadest market possible, each energy company is different and has different requirements at the detailed level. As a result, a vendor's standard packaged ETRM software has to be designed to be extremely configurable and flexible allowing it to provide custom solutions based on a single common software package. Additionally, ETRM software actually incorporates a very broad amount of functionality from deal capture through to accounting. Developers have tended to solve this problem in a manner that makes sense to the designers as opposed to the users of the software. Finally, ETRM software developers have, until recently, been constrained by available technologies and architectures making integration difficult and screen design somewhat inflexible.

However, users continue to demand improved ease of use for their ETRM software. Several UtiliPoint surveys[5] of users have demonstrated that they are frustrated with the lack of basic 'blocking and tackling' in ETRM software which has many bells and whistles. In other words, they are frustrated that while the software provides all sorts of functions it has been assembled in a way that makes it difficult for the user's to utilize the software. This is reflected in both user's software procurement criteria (Figure 6.3) and in what user's tell us are their systems key weaknesses (Figure 6.4)

While the users specify 'ease of use' as a key buying criteria, many of their other key buying criteria such as 'flexibility', 'reporting', 'integration' and 'performance' are also usability issues.

Figure 6.3: User's buying criteria for ETRM software

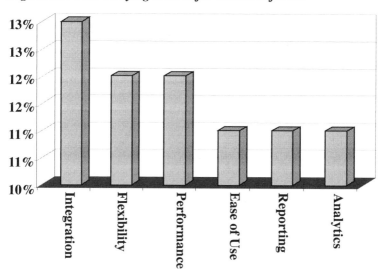

[5]ETRM Software Survey conducted by UtiliPoint, 2004. Unpublished.

Figure 6.4: User's views on ETRM system weaknesses

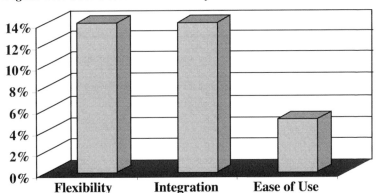

As Figure 6.4 demonstrates, the top three system weaknesses specified by users are also all essentially usability issues.

In part, the user's frustrations regarding ETRM systems ease of use is due to their backward looking nature. ETRM systems were historically designed to be data recording systems for particular business functions such as trade capture, risk management, logistics and accounting. Some element of process flow was incorporated to take a deal and process that transaction through the system to an invoice. But the software was often designed for a particular type of Energy Company and only as an afterthought was functionality added to cater for a broader market. To the end user, being forced to adopt the vendor's interpretation of business processes and data capture methods translates into inflexibility. As a result, their ETRM software is neither engaging to use or easy to learn and may, in fact, result in inefficiencies and reduced effectiveness.

New Technologies Offer Benefits

Today, new technologies and architectures such a Microsoft's .Net, web services and new user interface tools has provided ETRM software vendors and their users with the ability to address the usability issue. These tools allow vendors to offer solutions that provide significantly improved connectivity, scalability, flexibility and usability thereby increasing buyer's return on investment and reducing total cost of ownership. Additionally, as the ETRM software segment matures, vendors and users alike have learned from their past experiences and have placed usability as a both key design component and as a major buying criterion.

ETRM Reporting

An area of particular weakness in ETRM systems and solutions historically has been the reporting tools (see Figure 1). Many systems have provided users with some set of standard reports along with an ad hoc report generator. The issue with this approach as been that standard bundled reports are often too generic and need to be customized adding cost to system implementation while ad hoc report generators have required user knowledge of the underlying data structures to extract data and then provide only limited flexibility in terms of analysis of the data presented by the resulting report. Indeed, UtiliPoint has commented on this weakness many times in the past observing that even a $40 personal finance program has more reporting functionality than most ETRM software solutions. As a result, reporting has been an area of frustration for users and a tremendous source of revenue for independent consultants and the vendors themselves through the provision of report writing services.

Business Benefits of Usability

Usability increases customer satisfaction and productivity. Among the cited benefits is increased user productivity, decreased user errors, decreased training costs and decreased user support. In the complex world of ETRM software, there are also additional benefits to be gained.

Implementation of ETRM systems is difficult and costly. UtiliPoint surveys[6] demonstrate that even when implementations are 'successful', the users do not get to extract as much value from their investment as they expected because the system is unwieldy, difficult to use and doesn't exactly fit the requirements at a detailed level (Figures 6.5). In fact, many implementations are known to fail and there are many energy companies that have procured ETRM software that is today still sitting on the shelf.

[6] IT Benchmarking at North American Power Marketers, UtiliPoint International Report, 2004.

Figure 6.5: ROI for ETRM Software

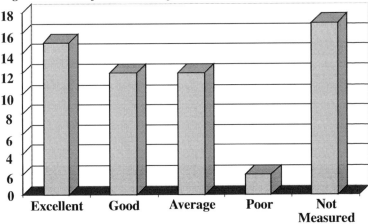

Source: UtiliPoint International Power Marketers IT Study, 2004

Part of the implementation issue is around usability of the software. Most often, implementations are suboptimal because users do not 'like' the software as it is inflexible, forces them to adopt new business processes, provides reports of limited usefulness and isn't very useful in helping manage the business. Indeed, the system becomes just a place to store data and is only as a rear view mirror. When a system is usable, the users are more likely to adopt it, learn how to extract value from it more rapidly and begin to use it as a management tool. It produces a return on investment as well as a lower cost of ownership.

Custom ETRM software delivered out of the box

This level of usability, configurability and flexibility provides the buyer with an essentially a supportable custom solution that meets its specific needs out of the box. Since each energy company that uses the packaged software can configure and set up the software to meet its business process, functionality and user preferences around display and reporting, each implementation has the ability to be a 'custom' implementation without increasing the cost, risk of complexity of the implementation or on going support of the software. Indeed, this particular issue is well on the way to being solved along with that of integration by virtue of new technologies such as .Net and web services, for example. We are now entering the era of forward looking ETRM software.

New development tools and architectures have provided the basis on which users can extract a better ROI from their investment in ETRM software solutions. Much of the benefits obtained from using state of the art ETRM software are to be gained from the increased usability that these systems can now offer. However, to be usable, the system must have been designed with the user at the center of the system (user centered design) as opposed to as a reflection of the vendor's view of the business.

Data Management

Another challenge facing IT staffs is data management. Maintaining accurate and timely data is a key activity that can reflect on the business in numerous ways from inaccurate financial reporting through to inaccurate billing and collection delays. Part of the issue is simply volume of data but an additional concern is data ownership. Much company electronic data is generated in individual business functions and stored in application-specific databases while masses of paper data may be filed across the company's departments. Not only is access to accurate data a key concern but reconciling the different versions of data across functions can prove to be both tedious and time-consuming.

In this regard, determining data ownership and "system of record" for data is key along with adherence to internal data management standards. Good data management not only improves the ability to extract timely value for the business to support decision making activities but it also assists in corporate governance efforts. Further, data management is an essential activity in supporting an energy company's brand through accurate and timely interaction with the outside world including customers, business partners and stakeholders.

The migration of IT architectures from the client/server model of the 90s to an n-tier, Web services and object-oriented world both helps and hinders the data management issue. By delivering increased and improved integration capabilities, these architectures are bringing the possibility of improved data management closer to reality. Conversely, the migration to these architectures can be a major undertaking and dependent upon the application vendors' own migration plans. Additionally, these architectures provide for improved business processes via embedded workflow and col-laboration.

Energy companies operating in today's North American energy markets face unprecedented uncertainties, not just in terms of market structural and regulatory changes, but also in responding to their own company's evolving and changing strategies. Indeed, the ability of IT departments to respond to the rapidly changing needs of the business is a major challenge and one that in success is taken for granted but in failure can have very negative implications. Agility has become a key word for IT professionals working in energy companies as they struggle to support business decisions against the backdrop of dynamic markets.

Today, most energy companies and utilities have reduced their IT staff numbers considerably but the demands on those who remain have increased significantly. While some companies have opted to outsource some or all of their IT needs in an effort to reduce costs and improve responsiveness, many continue to rely on their own IT

IT Responsiveness

One of the key issues facing energy companies and utilities is IT responsiveness. Business decisions to enter or exit regional markets, enter or exit different business and/or to acquire new assets or businesses are being made faster. For example, a utility seeking to enter retail markets in a region of North America or a pipeline company seeking to acquire add tional pipeline assets needs to be certain that IT can respond and deploy fast enough to actually support that business decision.

According to Robert Brassard, IT manager for EPCOR Merchant & Capital, new technology deployments are a component in building IT responsiveness. His company has undertaken a series of initiatives around desktop operating systems and the introduction of Java for example. However, Brassard's IT group also routinely performs "what if" studies resulting in discussion white papers to consider approaches to take if a certain business event occurs and through contingency planning to pre-build strategies and project plans for projects that might be triggered by a business event. "The challenge is to see how we can get from zero to 100 mph in 60 days from an IT point of view to support a particular business initiative," he says.

Another strategy used by EPCOR Merchant & Capital IT is to be fully engaged with the businesses through a relationship manager who works with business line managers. "Having IT staff closely engaged with the business keeps us aware and knowledgeable while facilitating a conversation that engenders mutual respect," he says. He cites one example of a project where there were less than 12 weeks to deliver the IT components required to allow the business to move into a new regional market. "We were prepared with contingency plans, qualified and competent staff, and available and pre-qualified external vendors who had the right experience."

One issue cited by Brassard is keeping up with and being aware of players in the market in terms of available solutions and technologies. "This is a challenge especially for smaller IT departments. Our approach is to bring in qualified outside assistance from firms such as UtiliPoint."

The Importance of Architecture in IT Responsiveness

Although there are strategies such as those used by EPCOR Merchant & Capital to help IT respond to the business in a timely fashion, Brassard also emphasizes the importance of IT architecture in gaining the "nimbleness" required to respond quickly. Indeed, EPCOR Merchant & Capital IT is now forced to be "on par" with technology and architecture by the demands of the business. "In a regulated world we could afford to use legacy systems because no one was forcing us to extend. Now we are also playing in non-regulated environments where we have to support the business in a rapidly changing environment, we are pushing the boundaries of technology and have to bring in the most flexible architectures that allow us to respond effectively," he says.

Fortunately, the tools and technologies are now available to provide the flexibility, scalability, performance and connectivity required and they are available at a price point and learning curve that is acceptable. Similarly, many application vendors across the utility space have migrated or are migrating their own offerings to new technologies and architectures in line with market demand.

At the heart of IT responsiveness in the energy and utility industry is the need to deploy architectures and tools that can facilitate more rapid deployment of solutions at reasonable cost. While the architecture does not by itself provide responsiveness, it is the central player in an IT strategy and approach that does. As the pace of business increases in an already volatile energy business, companies that lag in the deployment of flexible IT infrastructures will find themselves unable to respond to these business challenges. Similarly, application vendors that do not or cannot migrate their products to more modern platforms will increasingly find themselves unable to provide their solutions at the right price point and over the timescales demanded by energy companies.

Faced with both heterogeneous legacy software environments and poorly-integrated systems, IT departments are confronting a serious challenge. IT staffs are too often stretched thin simply dealing with routine "support and maintenance" issues to find the necessary resources and time for the planning that is required to properly support future business initiatives and industry changes.

Streamlining the Flow of Information in an Energy Marketing Organization

Every CFO wants more information about the impact of trades as early as possible. Every CEO needs to be able to back up the valuation of his organization by showing a consolidated view of the book of business. The CRO needs to be able to certify that all trading data is accurate, and every VP of Trading wants to be sure that there will be no ugly surprises in the company's trading position. These four demands are continually driving changes in the IT infrastructure within trading organizations. Unfortunately, realizing solutions to these demands is a non trivial exercise.

During the boom years up until 2001, energy trading and marketing companies viewed IT as a competitive advantage with companies spending significant amounts of money on leading edge solutions. Enron led the way with a reputed spend of 11 percent of revenue spent on IT. During the past five years expenditure on IT solutions has significantly reduced, and the emphasis has shifted from competitive advantage to defense (i.e., Sarbanes-Oxley) and must haves (i.e., what systems do we need in place to run the business). The four demands of the CEO, CFO, CRO and VP of Trading have mandated point solutions for the most part that do not work in concert.

Alternative Approaches

There is a constant tension between the "monolithic" solution from a single vendor that solves all problems and provides a consolidated view to the corporation, and the alternative "best of breed" approach that stitches together solutions from different vendors. Both solutions have their merits and downfalls.

The "Monolithic" Solution

The "monolithic" solution attempts to avoid the pitfalls of attempting to integrate multiple point solutions by providing a single solution to all the major categories of applications in one software offering. This is nice in theory, however, the solutions required by energy companies are extremely complex, and the market for customers that can afford such a solution is relatively small. Internally developed projects often tend to end up pursuing more of a "monolithic" approach.

Vendor companies that offer the "monolithic" solution tend to rely heavily on a services model to augment the license fees and support contracts. The services they offer tend to build custom installs at each new implementation which in turn drives up both the implementation and maintenance costs. Companies offering "monolithic" solutions depend heavily on a broad base of Support and Maintenance revenue to invest in R&D. Once the base of Support and Maintenance revenue falls too low, or if it never gets high enough, then the vendor is forced to go to investors and / or the customer base for additional investment to roll out new versions. This usually is a precursor to some M&A activity on the horizon.

Best of Breed Solutions

Best of breed solutions are on the face of it a great option for all involved. Customers get the benefit of niche products that directly solve their problems, and vendors don't have to support the expense of a massive code base associated with the "monolithic" system. However there are problems with the best of breed approach too. Namely, the customer now has several silos of information that must be massaged and reconciled continually to get any semblance of a smooth business process, and all results must be continually reconciled in order to check that results are accurate. To make matters worse the IT integration expenses tend to be horrendous with popular rules of thumb putting this at 45 percent of an IT budget. For vendors, the situation can be very difficult because they don't have a solution that solves enough of the customer's problems, and so either get left out of customer selection processes and / or get continually pushed toward creating a "monolithic" solution.

Developments

Fortunately advances in technology have moved forward significantly since 2001 and the modern trading and marketing organizations can have their cake and eat it too with some forethought and planning. Examples such as web services and Service Oriented Architectures (SOAs), when combined with XML standards, come to mind. These technologies when combined with professionally built ETRM solutions enable customers to build the solution to answer the "C" level demands without the overhead and risks of the "monolithic" solution.

In reality the ground work for a lot of the capabilities that exist today were in place and being utilized by companies such as Enron and Dynegy leading up to the 2001 meltdown. Specifically, middleware products such as TIBCO and Vitria enabled the first baby steps in the right direction.

However, these projects were hugely expensive and implementation came at a considerable risk of failure. The resulting projects, if successful, tended to be a custom, one off build and did little more than smash the spaghetti of integration interfaces through a middleware bus rather getting rid of the spaghetti and the associated expenses and complexities.

Several of the major oil and gas companies have very advanced solutions in this area today and continue to invest in global solutions to drive efficiencies for their organizations.

Suggestions for Ways Forward

In order to undertake a solution to take advantage of best of breed solutions without the resulting "spaghetti overhead," there are several steps that can be undertaken:

1. Get buy in and commitment from senior management. This will not be a six-month short-term project, but rather it will be a long term infrastructure investment in the future of your company. It will bear fruit many times its' cost.

2. Choose a good middleware product that

   • can support the traffic that will be generated by your organization

   • supports your choice of interfaces between systems (do you go with .NET or with JAVA)

   • is provided by a vendor that will be there tomorrow to support your organization. You are making a major decision on this piece of technology and this should not be taken lightly since it will become the core of your ETRM infrastructure.

3. Spend significant time up front planning how the end point applications will communicate with each other. Not the transport component, which should be provided by the middleware vendor, but rather the exchange of information. For example, getting a risk management system to communicate deals with a physical transaction management system is a non trivial exercise, and this is an n2 problem. In other words, the more systems you have to integrate the more planning you need to do.

4. Select ETRM solutions on an ongoing basis that support your vision of the "straight through" organization. Any vendors or providers that will not support your choice of interface technology cannot be considered.

5. Choose early wins. The big bang project will lose support early on. It is far easier to choose some simple trading exchange integration projects then to bite off the SAP to (Insert the ETRM solution of your choice) integration project as your initial project.

Conclusion

Change is the only constant; as UtiliPoint® research has shown ETRM systems are changed out more often than most other corporate systems; regulations change; business models change. What doesn't change however is that the senior executives of energy trading companies must deliver for their shareholders and keep themselves out of trouble in the process. This all requires technology and architecture to support the corporation. Luckily we are at a point where the technologies exist to make this a feasible with some diligent forethought, commitment and planning.

The Emergence of the ASP Model

According to Internet.com's webopedia definition, an ASP is "a third-party entity that manages and distributes software-based services and solutions to customers across a wide area network from a central data center." The ASP model usually provides a software solution that is hosted remotely and accessible over the internet. To be a viable candidate for ASP delivery, the hosted software solution needs to have broad applicability to prospective users and so it usually delivers a set of fairly standard functionality. The delivered solution can still provide configurability to allow users to set up business processes and workflow but to gain the economies of scale and cost, it must be a single solution utilized by many different users. Users generally pay a monthly usage fee for access to the software. In the ERM category, only a small number of 'ASP' solutions actually fall into this category including, SunGard Kiodex' Risk Workbench solution.

Indeed, many of the traditional vendors have been quick to see the ASP as a model for delivering their software solutions on a different pricing basis. However, many of these 'ASP' solutions are in reality a customized version of the existing software solution hosted by the vendor specifically for a single user client and in that sense, they are not true ASP solutions but are in reality a traditional software package hosted for a single client.

What are the Benefits of ASP delivery?

There are a number of benefits of true ASP delivery of ERM solutions. These include costs, risks and implementation benefits. Since an ASP solution is essentially shared by a number of users (though data is effectively partitioned by client) it can be provided at a much lower cost than a traditional solution, usually for a monthly usage fee. However, it is the lack of a software implementation that provides the true cost benefits of an ASP solution significantly reducing the entry price for a professionally developed, ERM third-party solution. Implementation is limited to a short period of user training since the application is hosted remotely at the provider's site.

Traditional software implementation is often the largest cost associated with packaged software, especially ERM software which is highly configurable and therefore often complex to implement. In a traditional implementation hardware is required to be purchased and supported by IT staffs, key users are required to be involved in the implementation for an elongated period with both a direct cost element as well as an opportunity cost to the business, and a systems integrator and/or vendor team is required on site at consulting rates. As a result, implementation costs can be anywhere from 1 to 6 times the cost of licensing the software package.

Implementation projects are also a source of risk. It is well established that IT projects have high failure rates and the larger and more complex the project, the more that risk increases. Indeed, historically, ERM implementation projects have a high risk of failure as shown by the replacement cycle for ERM software of once every 4 years (compared to, for example, Customer Information Systems' replacement rates of once every 10 years)[7]. With an ASP solution, there is usually no implementation or that implementation is drastically reduced in size, cost, risk and scope to essentially data conversion and loading activities.

An additional benefit which should not be underestimated in the volatile energy industry is that all upgrades and maintenance releases of the software are performed by the vendor. ERM software requirements often move so quickly that vendor's are forced into numerous annual releases. Each release requires the users to re-test the software in a test environment and then to perform the upgrade in the production environment. The costs and risks associated with maintaining multiple environments are eliminated with ASP solutions where the vendor provides this service at their own site and the cost and risk of the upgrade activity is also eliminated.

In summary, the true ASP model provides a fully functional, flexible solution at a fraction of the cost and risk of traditional software license procurement reducing the barriers to entry in to a professional solution for smaller operations and start ups alike. At the same time, the client is up and running on the solution in a matter of days not months and without the need for specialist IT staffs and extra computing equipment.

[7]Source: "IT Benchmarking of North American Power Marketers" report by UtiliPoint International, 2004

Where Does ASP Really Work?

Plainly, an ASP provided ERM solution is not necessarily the best solution for all energy industry participants. So what types of entity and in what circumstances might an ASP provided solution prove to be most applicable?

Firstly, an ASP ERM might be considered by start-up energy trading operations that want a professional software solution in place at the start, even if they plan to migrate over time to a more traditional licensed solution. In today's business environment of corporate scrutiny and compliance, spreadsheets are too open to error, abuse and mistakes to be utilized in energy trading while an ASP solution provides the security of access, accountability, auditability and reporting needs that a spreadsheet solution cannot.

However, the ASP ERM solution is ideal for both speculative traders and smaller energy enterprises such as hedge funds, banks, pension funds and commercial & industrial end users for example. For speculators, the ASP solution provides an energy-specific solution for capturing trades, managing and reporting risks and for financial reporting. For commercial & industrial companies (such as airlines, School districts etc.) that are procuring fuel or trading excess generation, the ASP platform also supplies all of the necassary energy-specific requirements. A third potential user that can benefit from the ASP solution are smaller physical players such as municipal and cooperative utilities were the scale of operation does not make licensing ERM software a cost effective proposition.

Table 6.1: Summary of Candidates for ASP ERM Solution

Scenario	*Candidates*
Start-up trading entity	Any entity entering the energy trading industry. ASP solution utilized instead of spreadsheets or other custom-built applications as an interim solution. Ensures business and workflow controls, minimizes potential for errors and abuse, requires security of access, provides audit trails and adequate risk and financial reporting.
Speculative traders	Speculative traders including but not limited to hedge funds, pension funds, endowment funds, investment banks etc. Require energy-specific function-ality in deal capture and risk reporting combined with secure access, audit trails and compliance reporting.
Commercial & Industrials	Airlines, plants, School districts etc. procuring fuels and/or trading excess generation or hedging. Provides energy-specific functionality as well as financial and risk reporting.
Smaller Energy companies	Municipal Utilities, Cooperative utilities, smaller marketers, Generators, IPP's and retailers. Require cost effective ETRM system.

In addition to the specific benefits outlined above, the use of an ASP-based ERM will eliminate many of the problems associated with poorly integrated systems and the use of spreadsheets and other user-built software tools (e.g. Access applications, flat files etc.). A recent survey of North American power marketers by UtiliPoint found that spreadsheets are a ubiquitous feature of trading operations and that more than half of those surveyed had manually or poorly integrated software supporting their business (Figure 6.6). The risk to any business involved in trading or simply procuring energy in today's volatile energy markets are high without adding the data issues and increased chance for error or abuse with spreadsheets or poorly integrated software. Often, spreadsheets are used as a substitute for expensive ERM software and associated implementation in smaller shops. Today, the ASP ERM is a far superior and extremely cost effective alternative to spreadsheets.

Figure 6.6: Spreadsheet usage in wholesale power marketing organizations[8]

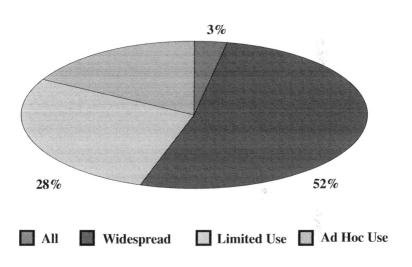

[8]Source: UtiliPoint International, 2004. "IT Benchmarking at North American Power Marketers' Report

SEVEN

SUCCESSFUL STRATEGIES FOR SELECTING AND IMPLEMENTING ETRM SOFTWARE

By Dr. Gary M. Vasey,
UtiliPoint International, Inc.

Software selection is, at best, a very subjective science. With so many vendors and offerings to choose between and, as many consultants willing to help, why do software selection exercises quite often end up as failed implementations? Time consuming and expensive for everyone involved, software selection appears to be a tricky business and one that rational people might do best to avoid.

Where to start?

The energy commodity trading and transaction management business is evolving and changing at a rapid clip and so are the available technologies and tools to support traders, schedulers and risk managers. By its' very nature, the energy commodity trading business is characterized by regional-ized, if not localized, constraints and differences as a result of both legislation and, due to the nature and geography of physical assets on the ground (pipes, wires etc.). Because of this, there is room for a large number of vendors selling software packages targeting this space – more than 65. And, although one or two of these vendors have become large and well known, in some cases, are now public companies open to more rigorous scrutiny, the vast majority still remain privately held and quite small.

For anyone at all familiar with the history of vendors and solutions in the energy commodities trading transaction and risk management market, there is an observable and consistent pattern of vendor dominance that those selecting software should be aware of. As one or two of vendors emerge and become more dominant gaining market share in the process, those vendors start to acquire other smaller vendors to gain functionality that they need for different geographies or types of user. The vendor is then usually faced with a major integration issue and has difficulty engineering a single product platform from their acquisitions. After a period of time, the vendors' need for cash outstrips their ability to generate it and, the effort spent trying to integrate diverse pieces of software reduces their ability to keep pace with market developments.

The end result is often that the vendor becomes an acquisition target itself for a new vendor that is enjoying greater sales success as a result of the market leader's inability to focus and generate revenue! Since the industry continues to evolve and adapt, new vendors are constantly emerging that are both ready and eager to take the place of those that fail to adapt.

It is therefore imperative to look carefully at all the vendors but particularly the smaller vendors. Indeed, it may well be that they have the superior product for your purposes. Additionally, new vendors are entering the market from Europe and other vertical trading markets such as financial trading. The market for software is simply too volatile to settle on looking at one or two of the larger vendors but it is mature enough to find useful packaged solutions.

With demand steadily increasing for ETRM software, more and more energy companies are facing the need to select new software. Set against a background of increased spending scrutiny, software selection projects—particularly those seeking ETRM software—carry an additional burden of responsibility for those tasked with managing the project. Indeed, since historically ETRM software replacement cycles have been somewhat more frequent than average for other software categories, companies may now be looking to replace older products and technologies to keep abreast with dynamic industry requirements.

Selecting software is never an activity that should be approached lightly. UtiliPoint research suggests that many ETRM selection exercises have taken place in the past without the necessary preparation and context, taking longer and costing more than planned as a result. The project will require proper project management through implementation and access to the best people in the company is needed on a consistent basis to ensure success. Use of an outside third-party should be considered to ensure that issues such as architecture and integration are properly addressed along with current and future business requirements. While this article cannot address all of the issues around software selection, here are four tips based on UtiliPoint's analysis and research that will help.

Start with Research

The first dilemma facing a project manager is how to compile a list of suitable vendors and products. With more than 65 vendors and products available in the software market, this is not an easy task. Additionally, the absence of a single definitive source for vendor and product information makes this task even harder. In the end, a search of the Internet and industry directories is often used.

While the temptation is to build a list of the better known vendors and products available, smaller and more obscure solutions should not be ignored at this stage. Industry complexity and variation in requirements between energy companies in different geographic locations, with different asset portfolios, and different reporting requirements, has essentially created an environment that supports a large number of diverse solutions, many provided by smaller vendors. A smaller, less well-known vendor may actually have the most suitable solution to meet your requirements and they should not be discounted on size alone. The starting list of vendors and solutions can be culled quite quickly based on a review of vendor Web site information and product collateral to arrive at a suitable, long list of vendors.

Tip 1: A little extra time spent performing vendor research, broadening the starting list beyond the better known vendors and solutions can result in a better selection and fit to requirements.

The Request for Proposal

Most energy companies utilize some form of Request for Proposal (RFP) or Request for Information (RFI). While many manage the project themselves, others utilize outside consultants to assist with the process and for help in building the RFP/RFI. Either way, building the RFP/RFI is a critical activity in the selection process requiring significant time and effort. Consideration should be given to a number of requirements in drawing up the RFP/RFI including:

• The actual functional requirements for each business process or set of business processes under consideration, at a reasonable level of detail. Additionally, it pays to understand whether the functionality is essential or simply nice to have. In building the requirements, consideration should be given to possible future requirements through an understanding of overall business strategy, plans and goals. For example, an electric utility may be seeking a system to manage its power transactions. All current generation may be coal-fired but if its plans include the possibility of building or procuring gas-fired generation in the future as a strategy, what impact might that have on requirements? Having to add natural gas functionality later to support fuel purchasing and management could be a significant expense. Equally, which markets is the company operating in and is that likely to change in the future? If so, does this impact the requirements in terms of a system's ability to interface with other market structures?

- System features and general business requirements ought to be considered including those requirements dictated by Sarbanes-Oxley, FAS 133. Features such as adequate security, audit trails, workflow and document management may also be required.

- IT infrastructure preferences need to be considered to ensure that the software can be cost-effectively supported internally and this category may include whether there is a preference for a traditional license or an application hosting model. It most certainly includes determining the need for integration with other existing systems.

- The vendor's track record, installed base size, culture and overall capabilities to keep the product current, should be taken into consideration when determining vendor preference.

If a third-party is used to help build the RFP/RFI, ensure that it is actually building your requirement set and not just tailoring a standard "cookie cutter" template. Standard templates may be a useful starting point but, in this industry, there is no standard set of requirements and using a "cookie cutter" approach will only result in extra work and cost along the way and in some cases, failure.

Finally, do be realistic about what you actually need in terms of a system and its capabilities by separating the "essential" requirements from the "nice to haves." Over-engineering the requirements will only increase costs and timescales and add to project risk.

TIP 2: Ensure that the requirements are properly understood in their broadest context, are realistic and workable and truly represent your company's requirements.

Reference Checking

Although ostensibly fairly obvious and intuitive, vendor reference checking sometimes simply does not occur in a selection project. References should always be checked and a little research can produce a number of additional references that can be checked in addition to those provided by the vendor. Turning up a poor reference should not necessarily preclude the vendor from further consideration although it is an additional risk element that has to be managed.

Reference checking provides valuable information about the vendor, the product and expectations. It can also turn up additional useful tips from a company that has already been through the process, helping to reduce or at least better manage implementation risk. If a poor reference is encountered, this should be addressed directly with the vendor as opposed to simply eliminating that vendor since all vendors have had poor implementation experiences and have unhappy customers. What is important is whether the vendor learned from the experience, whether that experience can be shared with you and how that has translated into better implementation procedures from which you will benefit.

TIP 3: Always check vendor references, both those provided by the vendor and those found through your own research.

Implementation

ETRM software packages are built by design to be both highly flexible and configurable. This configurability broadens the potential market for the software and can provide buyers with extremely useful capabilities from their software. However, configurability can also mean extra complexity to be managed during the implementation process. For this reason it pays to go beyond obtaining just a demonstration during the sales cycle from the vendor, who after all, if it has done its due diligence correctly, will have pre-configured its system for the sales situation. Asking for a hands-on demonstration will provide a better test of the software, a feel as to how the software works in practice and how easy it is to use.

As configuration usually takes place early in an implementation it also occurs at a time when the buyer is least familiar with the true scope and power of the software. In fact, incorrect configuration of the system can mean that work-arounds are later required to handle a particular requirement that the system might have been able to handle more elegantly if it had been configured correctly. Going back to reconfigure the software can be very expensive and in some cases may essentially involve a re-implementation.

Instead of immediately starting on the implementation, ask for training from the vendor and an extended hands-on environment in which key users can obtain proper exposure to the system. Unfortunately, users often only understand the true power of the software when it is too late and it is already configured and implemented.

TIP 4: Spend time learning and understanding the power of your selected software and matching it to your business before starting implementation proper.

The initial vendor list

The first dilemma faced by a manager tasked with finding the right software solution is to compile a starting list of potential vendors to consider. With 60+ vendors in the market, this is not an easy task.

The key in compiling the list is research. Simply compiling a list of the larger well-known vendors is insufficient since the solution that you are searching for may be offered by one of the smaller, less well-known vendors. This activity requires a comprehensive and coordinated search using such sources as your colleagues, the vendors, the Internet, industry directories and any other likely source that may help you compile the starting list.

The buyer's motivation will determine how well this research gets done:

- Do they view the decision as important and therefore worthy of a significant upfront research effort?
- Have they already a vendor in mind and just need two or three others to use as benchmarks?

Human nature being what it is, it's simple to take the easy way out and compile a short list of the better-known vendors despite the fact that to do so runs the risk of missing a potentially better solution.

Developing selection criteria

In order to successfully navigate through the selection process, it is imperative that the selection criteria are well understood, agreed and documented. These criteria need to extend beyond what is required from a functional point of view to include other considerations such as:

- The type of vendor and nature of that relationship
- Technology platform considerations
- Support capabilities of the vendor
- Ease of use and the ease of implementation in your business environment

And so on. Again, the answers here are not obvious but depend on the appetite for risk and reward of the buyer. It may be a good decision to buy software on a new technical platform from a small vendor if the initiative is likely to provide sufficient strategic advantage or ROI.

The next issue to decide upon is how will you go through the process and, will you use outside help? Does everyone on the team agree with the criteria and the process? Do you have the right level of commitment?

Here we meet another commonly cited reason for a poor selection decision - internal politics. Differences in opinion regarding the requirements or the process for selection, either at the beginning of the selection exercise or, one that develops during the process can result in the 'best laid' plans being abandoned in favor of power politics. Worse still, preconceived notions regarding a particular vendor or, even worse, actual experience (either a negative or positive experience) on the part of a vendor team member or the friend of someone on the team, can color the process right from the start.

The issue here is that vendors do learn from experience and often change for the better and sometimes, for the worse. To benefit from what a vendor may have learned through past experiences requires that they be allowed to present their case without bias. You must make your own assessment at that moment based on your own rigorous criteria.

How about outside help?

Many people asked to select software will naturally want to use outside help and expertise. Whether as a result of genuine need for help or sometimes, to have someone else to share the blame if the project goes off track. This is a popular way to get the job done. But wait. Doesn't the outside independent third-party experts that you hired have their own preferences and bias? How do you know that their motivations for selecting a particular vendor will truly reflect yours? For example, what if the independent experts lean toward a particular vendor because:

• They have an undisclosed relationship with the vendor,
• They have staff on board who have more familiarity with a particular vendor than others,
• They have friends working at that vendor,
• They used to work for the vendor,

• They too had a bad/good experience once with a vendor.

If you really sit back and actually examine the consultants' potential motivations, whether deliberate or unconscious, there is likely to be natural bias. It would be as well to understand that bias before beginning.

When using outside resources to assist in the selection process, you must remain responsible for taking the decision and should never delegate it to an outside party who may have reasons of their own for wanting to see a particular result.

What about the vendor?

Having done the required vendor research, the next step is to contact all of the vendors. A review of the information that they send will allow the elimination of many of them based on the selection criteria not being met and resulting in a short list. At this stage though, you may notice some striking similarities between their marketing materials. In fact, the only observable differences may be the logos and colors! This is the next problem faced by the selection team – differentiating between the claims and the counterclaims of the vendors.

To do this correctly would require an in depth demonstration of each vendor's software under carefully controlled conditions. As this is usually simply not an option, the process will naturally become somewhat subjective. Do you believe the vendor? What reasons can you think of to legitimately eliminate that vendor?

So, despite all attempts to keep the process on an objective basis, you are forced into subjective comparisons based on human perceptions. However, constantly referring back to the selection criteria and honestly assessing each vendor against those criteria may minimize the level of subjectivity.

The vendors' motivation is simple. It is to make a sale and keep the cost of that sale to a minimum. It is not usually the vendors' intention to mislead but their claims certainly need to be tested. Most often, vendors will promote planned features and functions, a legitimate marketing tactic if that functionality is to be delivered in the near future but one that carries a risk for the buyer that needs to be properly assessed. Has the vendor got a track record of delivery of new functionality in a timely manner?

Another area that requires close scrutiny is the vendors' use of terminology including: 'integration'. 'stp', 'risk management', 'VaR'. It is easy to make incorrect assumptions based on what the project team believes the vendor means by a term like 'integrated' when in fact the vendor means something quite different.

There are three excellent ways to test the vendors and their claims and surprisingly, some of them are often not used at all by the selection team:

1. Have the vendors respond to a pre-prepared Request For Proposal in a formal manner,
2. Have them demonstrate their solution,
3. Check their references.

Request for Proposals

The vendor's response to an RFP, much like the content of their marketing material cannot be accepted at face value. It is not that the vendor intends to mislead simply that they will put their best face forward. Often the RFP will contain template components that may be old or make statements that perhaps were once correct but are now not so. The obligation of the project team is to scrutinize the RFP and to test claims and terminology as best they can.

An obvious behavioral issue here on the part of the project team is the natural human willingness to accept statements at face value and to look for the answers that were both expected and desired. Caution is required as well as attention to detail to ensure that this natural and normal bias is balanced with the due rigor that needs to be attached to a decision of this importance.

The Software Demonstration

By all means have the vendor demonstrate their proposed solution. Use the demonstration to validate functionality and capabilities as well as to understand how well the software supports the current or planned business processes. Again, the vendor will naturally desire to present the best picture that they can to the selection team and so it is quite safe to conclude that the demonstration represents a better than normal usage situation.

Plainly, if the vendor arrives unprepared, unrehearsed and the fails to give a convincing demonstration, it should be expected that things will only get worse from there and the vendor should probably be discounted. The vendor's motivation is to prepare, prepare and plan their demonstration to the point that it goes smoothly and shows both them and their software to the best possible degree. Again, it is only human to assume that the demonstration experience will be repeated in real world use. This may well not be the case!

Reference Checking

Of all the methods to find out about your pending partner, this is by far the best. However, it is stunning how many companies selecting software never ask for references or, if they do, fail to check them. Remember, the vendor must be expected to provide only their best reference sites and so you should not be surprised to receive favorable responses. Of course, if the references are checked and unfavorable, then this should be a major red flag.

Checking references should not stop there. It is very easy to find out where else a particular vendor is installed. Simply check old press announcements, talk to colleagues and ask the vendor. It is imperative that other sites are checked too! A poor implementation or two is not necessarily indicative of the vendors' suitability but certainly provides a perspective of likely risks and vendor shortcomings to be expected.

ETRM Software Selection and Implementation - The Need to Prepare

Many companies fail to prepare properly for an ETRM software selection project. Integration and architecture are always a key component in an ETRM software selection project. UtiliPoint found that companies use between 8 and 12 separate applications to support wholesale power trading, transaction and risk management activities and that around half of those companies relied on manual interfacing between those applications. It is therefore important to determine the overall strategy to software selection at the beginning. Will you use a best of breed approach selecting a number of applications that then need to be integrated or will you seek a single vendor solution where some modules may not reflect your requirements perfectly but integration is already provided for?

In the latter case, UtiliPoint's survey also concluded that often the vendor provided functionality was not fully utilized and that companies needed to supplement the vendor software with custom components and/or spreadsheets. This particular issue is often related to poor selection choices as a result of imperfect preparation or a poorly conducted implementation project or both.

ETRM software is often highly configurable. This means that the software can be modified easily for many business situations. However, it also means that the software can appear quite complex and that many implementation decisions face companies implementing this type of software. Those decisions often get made at the beginning of an implementation project when the company is not familiar with the full power of the software it has purchased. Once the software has been configured it is not easy or cheap to go back and correct configuration mistakes. Proper preparation can help reduce these types of issues.

Expectation Setting

The aim of any software selection project is to procure software that meets the needs of the business. As a result, it pays to understand what those business needs are today and out into the future insofar as it can be known. The complexity inherent in ETRM software selection and implementation is related to the fact that the requirements are driven by the commodities traded, the assets employed in the business and the regulations governing the business in the geographies in which the business currently operates. So, for example, if the business might be seeking to expand into new geographies or acquire new assets, this needs to be built in to the requirements.

In terms of expectation management, preparation involves effectively communicating to senior management and other key staff what it will realistically take to successfully undertake the project in terms of;

• Budgets
• Staffing
• Management commitment
• Solution architectures and integration, and
• Users understanding and buy in.

Staffing for the project can be an area of difficulty. The project will require that the best resources in the company are deployed meaningfully to the successful selection and implementation. This may mean that there is an opportunity cost to the business and, without proper preparation and effective communication, these key staff are pulled in multiple directions and are unable to assist in the project properly. Fatal mistakes can be made if this situation arises. Of course, internal staff can be supplemented by outside help. The outside consultant can bring a wealth of experience to the table that will help streamline the project and reduce risks.

Finally, prepare your management. Management buy in can drive the success of the project and without it, the project will almost certainly fail. Identify the management champion for the project and ensure that they fully appreciate the demands the exercise will place on the organization.

Educating the Team

To some extent education and preparation overlap but proper education can greatly improve the success of an ETRM selection project. Education includes taking the time to properly research the universe of solutions and vendors available in the market place. Keeping current with vendors is a full-time job as the market moves rapidly and there are so many vendors. Recently for example, many of the leading vendors have migrated to new architectures on an n-tier platform with web services providing greater scalability, connectivity and configurability.

A third-party can conduct vendor and product research for you reviewing each vendor's solution set and capabilities and matching them to your overall requirements. By utilizing the third parties experience and research capabilities, the list of possible solutions can be narrowed rapidly to a smaller number of vendors who have a realistic capability of meeting your requirements. This reduces project costs and risks while ensuring that the project staff is not bothered unduly by calls and inquiries from all of the vendors.

Vendor Issues

There are a number of areas where the vendor needs to be tested more exhaustively. For example, reporting from the system. Reporting is a historical weakness of ETRM solutions which often arrive with template reports that do not meet your needs. The vendor will then write custom reports for you adding additional unexpected costs to the project. Look carefully at the reporting side of the software and what will be required to obtain the reports that your organization needs. Additionally, ensure that the software is truly configurable and isn't really just a template that has to be built out on a custom basis for each customer. Configurability means that the system can be set up by an administrator to behave in certain ways. This should be transparent and not require any additional coding.

Vendor's want to win your business and to do so they may 'stretch' the truth. Comments such as 'It's in the next version' require a commitment in the contract. If the vendor claims certain functionality ensure that you observe it in the demonstration. Sometimes a requirement is communicated to the vendor at a certain level of detail and the vendor claims that it is included in the system. However, at crunch time, the vendor's interpretation of the requirement is somewhat different in detail to the buyer's resulting in a mismatch. Always test vendor claims and that you communicate requirements in sufficient detail as to validate their claims.

As regards technology, the vendor ought to be on an n-tier platform today and should be using standard software and databases. Proprietary languages and software simply add unwanted cost and complexity and client/server technology is yesterday's technology.

Finally, vendors need to explain their upgrade policies. In an industry where the requirements can change rapidly, vendors are often forced into releasing multiple upgrades every year. This means that, in order to obtain that functionality, your organization will need to take those upgrades. If you have a single vendor, that may be manageable but if you select solutions from multiple vendors, it can become a maintenance nightmare as each vendor pushes out 4-5 upgrades a year. Additionally, find out and examine how upgrades are tested. Your organization will certainly need to have a complete test environment and an ongoing commitment to adequate testing scenarios and programs internally prior to deploying the software in a live business environment. ETRM initial software quality is not as good as other software categories in our experience. Again, you should allow for the ongoing testing requirements in your budget and resource planning.

EIGHT

EMISSIONS TRADING – THE COMING CLASH OF TWO SOFTWARE MARKETS

By Dr. Gary M. Vasey,
UtiliPoint International, Inc.

With the launch of the European Union Emission Trading Scheme (EU ETS) early in 2005, energy companies, along with other CO2 emitters, have entered a new world of complexity. From now on, energy companies will need to deal with carbon dioxide and other emission issues in the context of both their operations and their financial reporting. For energy companies with generation facilities, the EU ETS has an impact on day-to-day operations, long-term planning and potentially on shareholder and analyst sentiment.

Carbon is now expected to become a truly global commodity market much in the same way as crude oil. Estimates vary on the potential financial value of global carbon markets from around $10 billion by 2005[9] to as high as $2.3 trillion of trades by 2012[10]. Despite the varying estimates, there is consensus that there will be a significant expansion in carbon markets by 2012. According to Fusaro & Yuen[11], the carbon market is now at a stage in its evolution similar to that of the oil markets before 1978. However, with the emergence of cap and trade schemes such as the EU ETS, the market is set to build rapidly as carbon dioxide becomes a fungible commodity trading market.

Despite the fact that the United States has declined to sign up to the Kyoto Protocol, emissions trading is already underway in certain U.S. states in both nitrogen dioxide (NOx) and sulfur dioxide (Sox), for example, using cap and trade programs. In fact, carbon dioxide trading is

[9]World Bank estimate in Miller, Nedia. Environmental Markets: Trading Tools and Financial Instruments. In: Fusaro, Peter & Yuen, Marion (eds). GreenTrading: Commercial Opportunities for the Environment. GreenTrading,

[10]US Council on Foreign Relations estimate in (9) above.
Fusaro, Peter & Yuen, Marion (eds), GreenTrading: Commercial Opportunities for The Environment. GreenTrading, Inc., 2004.

11

also occurring in the United States through exchanges such as the Chicago Climate Exchange, although it is a young and immature market. The real issue with respect to the United States' non-ratification of Kyoto is that in today's global economy, U.S.-based energy companies cannot afford to simply ignore emissions. Firstly, many have operations in Europe and other regions subject to regimes such as the EU ETS and secondly, they have similar shareholders and investors that are increasingly focused on social responsibility and environmental issues. Consequently, U.S. energy companies could potentially feel the impact of Kyoto just as much as those energy companies based elsewhere.

For utilities with power generation facilities, the new carbon regime has very significant impacts from dispatch through asset valuation and optimization, risk management, and financial and regulatory reporting. This white paper will examine the nature of the new carbon regime, its impact on utilities and its effect on energy trading and risk management requirements.

The EU Emissions Trading Scheme (EU ETS) and other Emissions Reduction Efforts

Following the ratification of the Kyoto Protocol, the EU and its member states worked on establishing an EU-wide regional emissions trading scheme under the European Climate Change Program. The aim of this program being to find a cost-effective approach to the region's emissions reduction commitment. In July 2003, the European Parliament formally approved a Directive to establish an Emissions Trading Scheme (ETS) for greenhouse gases. Its objective was to establish an "up-and-running" system within the region by 2005 in preparation for the international emissions trading scheme which is set to begin in 2008. As of 1 March 2005, only three EU member states had actually met the legal deadline to complete the allocation of emission allowances, whilst only Denmark, Finland and the Netherlands had established operational registries by the target date[12]. The launch of the registries is a key component in the EU ETS' development because spot trading cannot start without them.

A Cap and Trade Market

The EU ETS is essentially a "cap and trade" market. Cap and trade markets set a target or "cap'" on total emissions levels and instead of forcing emitters to reduce emission levels down to a target level, permits

---

[12]EU Emission trading Deadline missed by most. Environment Daily, March 1st, 2005

to emit up to this cap are granted by the government. This provides companies with a choice of either meeting their emission target by reducing pollution to below their cap level or by the acquisition of emission permits from other companies that have already reached their goals. Any impacted company that is able to reduce emissions will create surplus allowances that it can either retain for future use or trade with other companies. A company that exceeds its limits will need to purchase additional permits to avoid being penalized. In the case of the EU ETS, a shortfall in emission allowances at the end of the year incurs a penalty set at 40 Euro per tonne in addition to the market purchase price. An emission trading program such as EU ETS is valuable because it puts a market price on the cost of emissions allowing companies to make informed choices among compliance options.

The EU ETS is also an installation based system that will initially only cover carbon dioxide at 12,000 facilities. Reduction requirements and trading involving other GHGs are expected to emerge after 2007. While the scheme is technically independent of the Kyoto Protocol, it has been designed as a compliance tool for the EU to meet its Kyoto emissions reduction target of eight percent below the 1990 level. It will be implemented in two phases between 2005-2007, and 2008-2012. Surplus allocations can be carried forward to the following year but only within the same "phase" meaning that current surpluses can only be carried over until the end of 2007, at which point they become invalid. The second phase is intended to coincide with the first commitment period of the Kyoto Protocol, and thus the EU has taken particular attention to ensure compatibility between any community scheme and the international emissions trading scheme under Kyoto.

All twenty-five EU member states will be able to participate in the emissions trading program; current estimates are that more than 12,000 installations from five sectors will be included, covering 46 percent of EU CO2 emissions. The five sectors are[13]:

• Power and heat generation (for installation with a rated thermal input exceeding 20MW)
• Mineral oil refineries and coke ovens;
• Production and processing of ferrous metals including metal ore, pig iron and steel;

[13]Evolution Markets (2004). "European Carbon Market Becomes Reality."

- Production of cement clinker, glass, tiles, bricks and porcelain; and

- Production of pulp and paper (for installations with production capacity exceeding 20 tons per day)

All member states must also have a registry in place in order to track emissions allowances. Transfer of allowances have to be notified to the registry and amounts of emissions produced each year must also be recorded and verified to surrender an equivalent amount of allowance certificates at the end of each year. So far, most countries have signed up to the UK or French registries, and only Austria has decided to develop its own domestic registry[14]. To date however, only a handful of European countries have actually launched domestic emissions trading schemes.

While trading has been dominated by OTC (over the counter) transactions, a number of exchanges have already emerged and many of these exchanges have close ties to the electric power markets. OTC transactions are likely to remain an important component in trade volume whatever occurs with respect to the exchanges. For power, spot markets are used primarily by industrials while futures are utilized by both industrials and financial players. In emissions, both banks and hedge funds have already entered the futures markets to speculate on prices bringing in additional liquidity. Today, forwards are primarily being traded because spot and futures markets cannot start until the national registries of the 25 member states are operating.

The ETS Directive also recognizes the use of emission credits gained through project-based, "flexible mechanisms" established under Kyoto. Under the EU's Linking Directive, carbon emissions credits from Joint Implementation (JI) and Clean Development Mechanism (CDM) projects will be able to be imported into the EU ETS. This has a significant effect on the development of emissions reduction projects around the world, which in turn also has an impact on the pricing development of carbon and EU allowances.

Other Emissions Schemes

Outside of the EU ETS, countries that have not ratified the Kyoto Protocol – most notably the United States and Australia – have developed some mandatory and voluntary regional emission trading programs. In the

[14]Point Carbon (2004). "Carbon Market Europe." November 26, 2004.

United States, the Bush Administration's decision not to ratify the Kyoto Protocol combined with the absence of federal regulations have hindered domestic efforts to develop a U.S. GHG emissions trading market. Additionally, U.S. reductions are not recognized under the Kyoto Protocol or the EU ETS, making it impossible to export U.S. emissions reduction credits to either of these systems.

The current status of the U.S. GHG market is both small and fragmented. There is a registry system in California and a carbon offset investment fund in Oregon. Only two states, Massachusetts and New Hampshire, have taken steps to develop state-level cap-and-trade systems. Both these state programs are still in the rule-making stage. Under the Regional Greenhouse Gas Initiative (RGGI), New England is likely to see its first regional GHG markets develop, a market that is largely driven by state and regional climate action plans that include the development of regional GHG reduction policies. The region is expected to launch its own regional registry system in the next one to two years, and a regional cap-and-trade system further down the road[15].

The lack of mandatory GHG reduction requirements in the United States means that voluntary programs as well as individual company commitments characterize the current market environment.

The U.S. carbon market is largely buyer driven, where a small number of companies, such as Entergy, DuPont and a few others, have been the primary driving force behind Verified Emissions Reduction credits (VERs) demand in the United States. VER buyers are generally motivated by individual or specific commitments to meet emissions reduction targets that have been made by programs such as the EPA Climate Leaders, DOE Climate Challenge or the Chicago Climate Exchange (CCX) program[16].

Impact of Emissions Trading on Utilities

Utilities are amongst the impacted companies under schemes such as the EU ETS by virtue of the polluting capabilities of their generation facilities and plants which are identified as "installations." As a result, the impact on

---

[15]Peter Zaborowsky and Jeffrey Reamer (2004). "Reality Check for the U.S. GHG Market." Evolution Markets Executive Brief, April 26, 2004. Edition 22.

[16]Ibid.

utilities or other energy companies with installations covered by the scheme is very broad. For example, it is estimated that the implementation of the EU ETS has created approximately EUR 15 billion worth of new assets and liabilities[17] in company financial reports. For the affected utilities, almost every detail of what they do is impacted by the new carbon regime.

The Broader Impact

The IFRIC, a committee of IASB, has decided that emissions allowances should be accounted for as intangible assets, in line with IAS38, whilst emissions are viewed as a separate contingent liability. This could potentially create accounting issues due to the "mixed model" which can cause volatility in a company's P&L account10. This volatility will need to be explained to investors. An additional accounting issue lies in determining the Fair Market Value of allowances. Under IAS20, allowances have to be recorded as government grants but they can be received at no cost and then traded for profit if unused. However, the market is still relatively illiquid with little price discovery to allow a fair market value assessment.

Additionally, in an era of socially responsible and environmentally aware investors, the Boards of impacted companies will need to pay close attention to environmental issues generally and provide strategy and directions for their businesses as a result. A significant part of this effort will be to ensure compliance with environmental regulations and to insure that the required systems and business processes are in place to do so. In the past, this has proven difficult to perform as a result of the plethora of state, federal and local regulations which can be both confusing and even contradictory. In that respect, schemes such as the EU ETS make it easier to comply since they are the result of a broader initiative.

For utilities with generation and plant assets, this means reviewing business processes and supporting systems in areas such as plant optimization, maintenance, health and safety, dispatch, valuation and financial performance. Optimization models now need to take into account the impact of the emissions cap and trade scheme as an additional factor to consider. A decision to generate now carries an additional cost in the form of having to potentially acquire an additional permit versus buying power in wholesale markets and selling any unused permits. This decision is made more complex depending upon the type of generation facility, its fuel

[17]No Smoke Without Allowances, Nicholas Neveling, Accountancy Age, 17th Feburary, 2005.

type and its emissions profile as a result of that fuel. Since the decision logic has become more complex, the emissions trading scheme may also have the desired effect of driving generators to cleaner generation where feasible such as hydro power. Indeed, the economics behind the development of new generation has also been impacted by the carbon regime now in place.

Additionally, a carbon regime such as EU ETS is likely to have an impact on the future price of power and potentially fuels too. These impacts now need to be included in generation modeling and planning as well as in the ongoing assessment of price and volume risk management and reporting. One might expect cost of the carbon regime to be reflected in forward power prices and, at some point in the future, to also impact the future price of fuels such as coal, natural gas and crude oil by discounting the price of cleaner fuels over those that create a larger emissions problem. Similarly, power generated using renewable or environmentally friendly facilities (green power) is already in demand and can attract a premium price.

The Impact of Compliance

More specifically, utilities will need to comply effectively with the EU ETS scheme by signing up with the appropriate registry and reporting back correctly. Additionally, the utilities will need to measure and forecast emissions from each plant in a verifiable and accurate manner so that optimal dispatch decisions can be made. This will ensure sufficient permits to cover its emissions for any vintage in order to avoid not just penalties but also public discernment issues around its profile in the market and brand. Tracking and understanding emissions position allows good decisions to be made regarding trading excess allowances in the market at a favorable time and price. As a financial market for emissions opens up, utilities may also seek to engage in hedging activities to offset emissions exposure.

Ultimately, these companies will need to ensure that the emissions position is also reflected accurately in their overall commodity portfolio and trading books. They will need to understand, track and report those exposures in the course of normal risk reporting and they will require trading systems to support and track their emissions trading activities. They will need an emissions trading and risk management system that provides the specific functionality required as well as the ability to provide portfolio-wide views of their entire position.

To that end, utilities will need software that provides the required functionality. They will be faced with two types of prospective software vendors – energy trading and risk management (ETRM) software vendors and environmental compliance vendors. The environmental compliance software market is still a relatively immature category with numerous small vendors. Additionally, while many offer the ability to measure, monitor, forecast and report emissions, in reality they lack the true trading and risk management capabilities that are needed. More importantly, they lack the ability and the experience of integrating with other systems such as generation dispatch, generation optimization and energy commodities trading, scheduling and risk management systems. On the other hand, while the ETRM vendors may lack emissions trading or tracking and risk management-specific functionality, they have the framework and configurability to add this functionality in a relatively short timeframe.

A further issue to consider with these software vendors is whether their software is targeted at the physical or financial side of the energy business. This is a key consideration for a utility with generation assets. Many ETRM vendors originated in the financial markets and as a result already lack the ability to model the complex behavior of generation facilities (such as mixed fuels, variable efficiency rates, etc) or retail customers correctly. This behavior is made more complex by the addition of emissions.. What utilities dealing with EU ETS and similar schemes require is a trading and risk system that was designed to cater for the physical specifics and complexity of their business.

Summary

Utilities are particularly impacted by emissions trading regimes and the consequences of non-compliance or poor decision making can result in serious consequences. Indeed, the reputation of the company is at stake since this is both an emotive and politically sensitive issue. To truly manage the impact of emissions, utilities need to be able to understand the true cost of their participation in the scheme while managing their exposure to optimize emissions allowance trading opportunities and to avoid penalties. From a strategic standpoint, the implementation of EU ETS essentially changes investment decisions. For example, what is the cost of trading emissions for a plant versus investing in new and cleaner facilities? Is it more cost effective to procure needed power in wholesale markets as opposed to firing up a 'dirty' peaking unit? All of these decisions require that the utility has a good assessment of its positions and costs.

APPENDICES

Energy trading, transaction and risk management vendor list

Abacus Solutions, Inc.
24704 Voorhees Drive
Los Altos Hills, CA 94022
650.941.1728
www.abacussolutionsinc.com

Advanced Reality, Inc.
2001 Hermann Drive
Houston, TX 77004
713.533.5839
www.advancedreality.com

Algorithmics Incorporated
185 Spadina Ave
Toronto, Ontario M5T 2C6
CANADA
416-217-1500
www.algorithmics.com

Allegro Development Corporation
1445 Ross Ave., Ste. 2200
Dallas, TX 75202
214-237-8000
www.allegrodev.com

APX Inc.
5201 Great America Pkwy
Ste. 522
Santa Clara, CA 95054
408-517-2100
www.apx.com

Ascend Analytics
Suite 100
976 Utica Circle
Boulder, CO 80304
303.415-1400
www.ascendanalytics.com

Axiom Software Laboratories Inc.
67 Wall St 8
New York, NY 10005-3101
212-248-4188
www.axiomsl.com

C Square
750 Terrado Plaza
Suite 229
Covina, CA 91723-3419
 626-653-0654
www.c-square.com

CalSoft Systems
6800 Koll Center Parkway
Suite 100
Pleasanton , CA 94566
925-249-3000
www.calsoft.co.in

Core Energy Solutions, LLC
P.O. Box 130290
Houston, TX 77219-0290
713-278-CORE (2673)
www.core-energy.com

Data Management Solutions
707 Hunters Creek Way
Hockley, TX 77447
713-408-7835
www.dmshouston.com

Decisioneering, Inc.
1515 Arapahoe St., Ste. 1311
Denver, CO 80202
303-534-1515
www.decisioneering.com

Derigen Solutions, LLC
591 North Avenue
Suite A / Second Floor
Wakefield, MA 01880
781-245-8141
www.derigen.com

DTN
9110 West Dodge Road, Suite 200
Omaha, NE 68114
800-485-4000
www.DTN.com

EnCompass Technologies
#1000 888 3rd St. S.W.,
Calgary, Alberta,
Canada T2P 5C5
(403) 237 7740
www.encompass-technologies.com

Energy Velocity
1495 Canyon Blvd Ste 100
Boulder, CO 80302
(720) 240-5500

Energy Softworx
12100 Race Track Rd
Tampa, FL 33626-3111
(813) 814-2550
www.energysoftworx.com

Energy Solutions International
13831 Northwest Fwy
Houston, TX 77040
(713) 895-7722
www.energy-solutions.com

Ensyte Energy Software
770 S Post Oak Ln Ste 330
Houston, TX 77056-1974
713-622-2875
www.ensyte.com

EnWorkz, Inc.
6101 Balcones Dr Ste 300
Austin, TX 78731-4277
512-323-9118
www.enworkz.com

Entero
324 8th Ave. SW, Suite 1300
Calgary, AB
Canada, T2P 2Z5
403.261.1820
www.entero.com

Epoch Energy Group
Two Allen Center
16th Floor
1200 Smith Street
Houston, TX 77002
713.658.1000
www.epochenergy.com

e-Systems.net, Inc.
P.O. Box 36114,
 Birmingham, AL 35236
205-991-1518
www.e-systems.net
www.attachesystems.com

Excelergy
10 Maguire Rd., Ste. 111
Lexington, MA 02421
(781) 372-5000
www.excelergy.com

Financial Engineering Associates, Inc.
(a wholly-owned subsidiary of Barra, Inc.)
2201 Dwight Way
Berkeley, CA 94704-2114
510-649-4640
www.fea.com

FNX Limited
225 Washington St Ste 300
Conshohocken, PA 19428-
484-530-4400
www.fnx.com

Fortech Software Consulting, Inc.,
4801 S. Lakeshore Dr. # 203
Tempe, AZ 85282
 480 237 0456
www.fortechsw.com

Global Energy
1470 Walnut Street, Suite 401
Boulder, CO 80302
720-221-5700
www.globalenergy.com

Infinite Software of Texas
20445 State Highway 249
Suite 290
Houston
TX 77070
281-320-8300 x300
www.infinite-software.com

Innovatix
Crossbow House,
40 Liverpool Road,
SL1 4QZ,
UK
44 (0) 8450531694
www.innovattix.com

IntercontinentalExchange, Inc. (ICE)
2100 Riveredge Pkwy
Suite 500
Atlanta, GA 30328
770.857.4700
www.intcx.com

Inssinc (Investment Support Systems Inc)
222 New Rd
Parsippany, NJ 07054
973-244-1661
www.inssinc.com

Intermark Solutions
307 East 53rd Street
6th Floor
New York, NY 10022
(212) 223 3552
www.intermarkit.com

Kase and Company, Inc.
18124 Wedge Parkway
Suite 405
Reno, NV 89511
(775) 853-7037
www.kaseco.com

SunGard Kiodex
3 New York Plz FL 15
New York, NY 10004
(646) 437-3900
www.kiodex.com

Lacima Group
501/25 Lime Street
Sydney NSW 2000
Australia
+61 (0)2 9299 4049
www.lacimagroup.com

Latitude Technologies
400 North Allen Drive Suite 302
Allen, TX 75013
972-747-1983
www.Latitudetech.net

LCG Consulting
4962 El Camino Real
#112
Los Altos, CA 94022
www.energyonline.com

Logical Information Machines (LIM)
120 North LaSalle Street
Suite 2150
Chicago, IL 60602
(312) 456-3000
www.lim.com

Lloret Data Systems Inc
14901 Quorum Dr Ste 525
Dallas, TX 75254
(972) 238-8126
www.lloret.com

Lukens Energy Group
2100 West Loop S Ste 1300
Houston, TX 77027
713-961-1100
www.lukensgroup.com

Murex
1270 Avenue of the Americas
Suite 1900
New York NY 10020
(212) 381 4300
www.murex.com

New Energy Associates, LLC (wholly owned subsidiary of Siemens Westinghouse Power Corporation)
400 Interstate N. Pkwy, Ste. 1400
Atlanta, GA 30339
770-779-2800
www.newenergyassoc.com

Navita Systems (formerly known as OM Technology)
25131 SE 42nd St
Issaquah, WA 98029-5790
425-427-9794
www.navita.com
www.omgroup.com

Nexant
101 2nd St FL 11
San Francisco, CA 94105
(415) 369-1000
www.nexant.com

Open Access Technology International, Inc. (OATI)
2300 Berkshire Ln N F
Minneapolis, MN 55441
763-553-2725
www.oatiinc.com

OpenLink Software, Inc. (OLF)
1502 EAB Plaza
15th Floor West Tower
 Uniondale, New York. 11556
(516) 227-6600
www.olf.com

PalmTree Business Solutions
1430, 335 - 8 Avenue SW
Calgary, AB CANADA T2P 1C9
Phone: (403) 264-6363
www.palmtreebreeze.com

Power Costs, Inc. (PCI)
3000 S Berry Rd Ste 100
Norman, OK 73072-7472
(405) 447-6933
www.powercosts.com

QuantRisk Corporation
Miami, FL
(786) 514-6600
www.quantrisk.com

Quorum Business Solutions (U.S.A.), Inc.
3010 Briarpark Drive,
Suite 450
Houston, TX 77042
Phone: (713) 430-8600
www.qbsol.com

Raft International
Piercy House, 7 Copthall Ave.
London
EC2R 7NJ, United Kingdom
+44-20-7847-0400
www.raftinternational.com

RCM Solutions, A division of Risk Capital Management Partners, LLCRisk Capital
1743 Wazee Street, Suite 250;
Denver, CO 80202
www.e-rcm.com

Reval
100 Broadway, 22nd Floor
New York, NY 10005
www.reval.com

RiskAdvisory (subsidiary of SAS)
610, 1414 - 8th Street SW
Calgary, Alberta T2R 1J6
(403) 263-RISK (7475)
www.riskadvisory.com

Rome Corporation
901 S. Mopac, Suite. 110
Austin, TX 78746
(512) 347-3200
www.romecorp.com

SAKONNET TECHNOLOGY
594 Broadway
New York, NY 10012
212 343 3170
www.sakonnettechnology.com

SAS
100 SAS Campus Drive
Cary, NC 27513-2414
(919) 677-8000
www.sas.com

Sisu Group
2895 E 89th St
Tulsa, OK 74137-3302
(918) 495-1364
www.sisugrp.com

SoftSmiths
2401 Fountain View
Suite 900
Houston, TX 77057-4804
(713) 626.9184
www.softsmiths.com

SolArc Inc.
320 South Boston Avenue
Suite 600
Tulsa, Oklahoma 74103
Toll-Free: 1 (888) 594-7320
(918) 594-7320 (outside the U.S.)
www.solarc.com

Spectrum-Prime Solutions L.P.
6750 West Loop South, Suite 500
Houston, TX 77401
713-662-8530
www.spectrumprime.com
info@spectrumprime.com

SunGard
Energy Solutions
1331 Lamar Street
Suite 950
Houston, Texas 77010
713.210.8000 office
713.210.8001 fax
www.sungard.com/energy

The Structure Group
2000 W. Sam Houston Pkwy. South, Ste. 1600
Houston, TX 77042
Phone: 713-243-7160
www.scgo.com

Tradecapture.com
1 Landmark Square
18th Floor
Stamford, CT 06901
(203) 327-7000
www.tradecapture.com

Trinity Apex
5001 Spring Valley Rd.
Suite 155 West
Dallas, Texas 75244
(214) 987-8900
www.trinityapex.com

Triple Point Technology
301 Riverside Ave.
Westport, CT 06880
(203) 291-7979
www.tpt.com

VisionMonitor Software, LLC
11451 Katy Freeway, Suite 510,
Houston, Texas 77079
713 935 0500
www.visionmonitor.com

ZE Powertools/ZE PowerGroup, Inc.
Unit 130
5920 No. Two Road
Richmond, BC
Canada
V7C 4R9
(604) 244-1469
www.ze.com

Please note: This list is believed to be correct at time of publishing. For an updated list and more information at any time, subscribe to the UtiliPoint Directory of ETRM Vendors and Products available at http://www.utilipoint.com/rci/details.asp?ProductID=1084

Other Useful resources

Other useful internet resources for those interested in ETRM software solutions, issues and suppliers include:-

www.etrmcommunity.com

www.utilipoint.com

UtiliPoint offers a Directory of ETRM Vendors and Products from its website. The directory is updated monthly with vendor news and quarterly with other vendor and software product information. The directory is available for subscription from UtiliPoint's website.

Additionally, UtiliPoint publishes a variety of free white papers and research for purchase at its website.

Sponsors Information

About Allegro

Allegro designs and delivers software that gives energy executives, operations personnel, traders and risk managers fully scalable, flexible solutions that are easy to integrate, deploy and modify—enabling companies throughout the energy industry to gain compelling advantages while keeping pace with volatile markets and emerging strategies.

Allegro advantages include more accurate understandings of market dynamics and risk, unprecedented efficiencies and collaboration among teams across the enterprise, full integration of physical product management and financial transactions, and more.

Allegro solutions provide customers with unbeatable advantages from the industry's only proven, modular component architecture and more than 30 best-of-breed energy application modules — all with seamless integration built from the ground up through Microsoft's .NET Web Services.

From its founding in 1984, Allegro has maintained a balance of evolution and innovation while providing customer-focused solutions that deliver a measurable return on investment. This approach has produced two decades of stable profitability, a rare achievement in a highly cyclical industry.

Allegro continues to deliver on its strategic roadmap and generate consistent growth as a privately held, self-funded enterprise — another energy industry rarity. As a result, the Company has been able to maintain a strong commitment to the long term needs of customers.

Now in its seventh major software generation in 21 years, Allegro serves large and midsize energy companies worldwide, upstream and downstream, from locations in London, Houston, Dallas, Calgary and Singapore. Its ever-expanding customer base includes the world's largest energy companies.

Contact Allegro at www.allegrodev.com or 214.237.8000.

About RiskAdvisory (A Division of SAS)

Acquired in 2003 by SAS, the world's largest privately-held software company, RiskAdvisory has completed engagements with in excess of 220 corporations, institutional investors, governments and other energy market participants. We offer risk management software solutions that are reliable, easily understood and provide clients with the ability to achieve best industry practice standards with respect to the capture, quantification and reporting of energy market and credit risk. Our global reach includes oil and gas companies, hedge funds, financial institutions, energy marketers and utilities companies.

Combining the strengths of RiskAdvisory and SAS, organizations can now achieve a holistic view with respect to data management, risk analysis and risk reporting. Our software solutions offer front office deal-capture capability for an expansive range of energy instruments and a powerful suite of risk analytics, giving companies the powerful risk management solutions they need to compete successfully in today's volatile energy markets.

For more information please visit www.RiskAdvisory.com. Contact us at RiskAdvisory@sas.com or call us at 403.263.7475.